BETWEEN TEACHER AND TEXT
Herbert Kohl, Series Editor

Teacher with a Heart:
Reflections on Leonard Covello and Community
Vito Perrone

TEACHER WITH A HEART

Reflections on Leonard Covello and Community

Vito Perrone

Teachers College, Columbia University
New York and London

Dedicated to
my mother and father,
brothers and sisters

Published by Teachers College Press, 1234 Amsterdam Avenue, New York, NY 10027.

Library of Congress Cataloging-in-Publication Data

Perrone, Vito.
    Teacher with a heart : reflections on Leonard Covello and
community / Vito Perrone.
        p.   cm. — (Between teacher and text)
    Includes selections from Covello's *The heart is the teacher.*
    Includes bibliographical references.
    ISBN 0-8077-3778-X (cloth : alk. paper). — ISBN 0-8077-3777-1 (paper :
alk. paper)
    1. Community schools—New York (State)—New York. 2. Community
and school—New York (State)—New York. 3. Covello, Leonard, 1887–
1982. 4. Teachers—United States—Biography. 5. Covello, Leonard,
1887–1982. Heart is the teacher.   I. Covello, Leonard, 1887–1982. Heart
is the teacher. Selections.   II. Title   III. Series.
LC221.3.N38P47   1998
373.19′09747′1—dc21   98-29612

ISBN 0-8077-3777-1   (paper)
ISBN 0-8077-3778-X   (cloth)

Printed on acid-free paper

Manufactured in the United States of America

08 07   8 7 6 5 4

Contents

BETWEEN TEACHER AND TEXT
Series Editor's Note

Creative work does not spring forth fully formed from the effort of a single individual. It is always built on the previous work of others, on their efforts, mistakes, insights, and struggles. This holds as much for education as it does for music, dance, theater, physics, and mathematics. This series is an attempt to connect present educators with their predecessors through imaginary dialogs and personal narratives. It is a way of showing the minds of current educators at work at the same time as providing a personal way to enter the history of educational thinking and practice. The goal of the series is to illustrate to teachers and people who want to become teachers that there are living traditions that are transformed by current practitioners. Hopefully it can provide creative connections that will encourage teachers to consider themselves intellectuals and historians, and reaffirm the importance of the teacher as a creative force in the making of education.

The series is also meant to encourage educators to become actively engaged with ideas - not merely with techniques, methods, and strategies but with thinking about children, learning, and the place of education in creating a decent world. Thinking about education and reading past works in the field should not merely be a necessity imposed by taking classes at teacher education institutions. It should be a part of one's life as a teacher and hopefully some of these books will provide models of entering into a continuing and creative dialog with some of the most inspiring and challenging writing about learning and schooling.

I have asked a number of educators to choose a person whose work has been important to them and enter into dialog with that work and by extension with that person. I have also asked them to chose an excerpt from that text which has moved them. Each volume in this series has an essay by a current educator and a selection from the text they are reflecting on. In this way the hope is that you can get a flavor of the original as well as a feel for how it helps shape current thinking.

Paulo Freire, the Brazilian educator, often talked about "reading the word and reading the world." For him reading in both contexts implies entering into dialog. In the case of a text this dialogic reading consists, among other things, of questioning the text, relating it to one's active moral, political, philosophical and personal concerns. It can involve doubting the text, incorporating it into ones thinking or action, rewriting it for current times, fantasizing the author answering questions raised about it, and wrestling to give it current significance. It is an active, participatory experience that makes a text come alive in the present.

The books in this series are an attempt to do just this - to show the life in a text through its current transformations. The essays are not critical analyses of the texts, exposition of their ideas, or accounts of their historical or educational importance. Rather they are explorations of the texts and the lives of the authors, acts of discovery that can lead to new ways of thinking through current problems through the wisdom of past educational insights.

Herbert Kohl
Series Editor

Preface

There are undoubtedly many different ways to respond to Leonard Covello and his autobiographical text, *The Heart Is the Teacher*. I could, for example, have taken several central ideas—immigrant students, intercultural education, advocacy for students and families, a curriculum of place, the community school—and shared my experience in relation to each, in this sense offering a more contemporary perspective. Another approach might have been to highlight as well as offer a critique of Covello's educational beliefs that continue to have important meaning for schools. I might also have engaged in a personal reflection on the central metaphor of the autobiography, "the heart as teacher," placing my autobiographical text alongside Covello's. In some respects, I have taken some of all three of these approaches, though wanting always to keep Covello's thought and actions paramount.

In focusing on particular aspects of Covello's work and educational commitments, I have consciously called attention to matters I believe should be thought about in the schools today. In the process, it may appear as if I am suggesting that we don't manage as well today, that Covello and his work are represented as an ideal. I start from the premise that work in schools, particularly in many of our less-advantaged urban and rural communities, is complex, often extremely difficult. Moreover, I don't subscribe to a belief in "golden ages," times when everything worked well. Covello's dispositions and practices were in his time exceptional, inspiring to many educators who worked with him and to many who knew him only through his writings and various accounts of his work in educational journals. But he was not alone in his day; there were many others who were also doing exceptional work. And there are many educators today who are doing equally impressive work. The larger point is that Covello raised in important ways central questions that we need to *keep* exploring. We have to keep our eyes on the students, their families, their neighborhoods, on what it means to educate for democracy, on the fullness of possibilities for our communities. It is too easy to be distracted from our central purposes as educators. When I question in this text "are we doing better?" or suggest "we are not so far removed today from what Covello described," I am trying to engage readers around the issues, provide something more to consider, not set up a "then and now," "better and worse" distinction. The history is more seamless than that.

Many of the issues educators are considering today have histories. They have been thought about before. Covello's book represents one of the important histories, a connection for us to another educator, one who thought deeply about the social and educational circumstances that surrounded him and remain close by. There is much in contemporary education literature, for example, about "the need to know the students." How do we think about this formulation? What are its meanings in our schools? Covello certainly understood the importance of "knowing the students," but he brought a considerably larger meaning to this understanding than currently exists in the educational discourse, one that we ought to reflect on and discuss. By confronting Covello's thinking and practice, we can enlarge our own thinking and practice. This is one of the benefits of remaining close to the history of our work as teachers and scholars, a means of keeping us connected across time and place.

Covello's story is explicitly urban, largely taking place in New York City's East Harlem, one of America's most densely populated and long most impoverished communities. Yet the account has meaning beyond such boundaries. Immigrant students are today in almost every community. The need to respect students is universal. The importance of schools' making connections to their communities, helping their students engage in genuine work, should resonate with teachers, students, and parents regardless of location. For example, one of the central tenets of the current Annenberg Rural Challenge, an effort to revitalize rural schools and communities, is, in fact, constructed around "a pedagogy of place." Covello's work is particularly inspirational to those involved in the Rural Challenge because he understood so well the need for students and families in communities to be closely connected through the work of the school.

The first part of this book is an extended reflection on Covello's autobiography; the second part presents extended portions of Covello's text, *The Heart Is the Teacher*, selections I thought would be especially interesting to contemporary educators because they relate to issues currently being debated in the schools. There is little overlap between what I have quoted in the initial portion of the book and these excerpts, and all page references in my essay are to the 1958 complete edition.

My hope in presenting my reflections and portions of Covello's autobiography is that our various educational conversations may become richer, that those of us who work in and around schools will be inspired to recommit ourselves to a wide-awakeness on behalf of our students, schools, and communities, to a greater understanding that we are about democratic work. Our schools are not yet as good as they should be. The need for reinvention is large. Covello's work offers us some important possibilities.

At present, the educational discourse is not, from my perspective, particularly inspiring. The language is heavily technocratic, filled with admonitions about the needs of "a global economy" and threats of failure. It is a view that looks right past the students, almost as if they aren't present. Everything is seen in an undifferentiated manner. Yet the universe that Covello committed himself to—first DeWitt Clinton High School and then Benjamin Franklin Community High School in East Harlem, both secondary schools exclusively for boys—were very specific schools in a clearly defined geographical space. The New York Public School System was far away from his ongoing concerns. In today's policy arena, Covello's educational commitments might well be viewed as peripheral, too exceptional. The work of Benjamin Franklin, the school Covello and a group of dedicated teachers created, would be seen as inconsistent with the need for all schools to be more alike in purpose, curriculum, and practice—part of the "scaling-up/systemic-reform" discourse that has become so dominant. Yet returning to Covello's educational stance, coming to understand the ways he and teachers in the Benjamin Franklin Community High School came to see their work, may help many educators look beyond the current discourse of scaling-up/systemic-reform, toward keeping a more powerful, more democratic educational vision within view.

This book has been enriched greatly by my ongoing conversations with members of the North Dakota Study Group. I also wish to acknowledge Jan Still, my staff assistant, for her help in the preparation of the manuscript.

Vito Perrone
Cambridge, Massachusetts

TEACHER WITH A HEART

*Reflections on Leonard Covello
and Community*

Reflections on Leonard Covello
and Community

Give me your tired, your poor,
Your huddled masses yearning to breathe free,
The wretched refuse of your teeming shore,
Send these, the homeless, tempest tossed to me,
I lift my lamp beside the golden door.

Emma Lazarus, "The New Colossus"

◆ 1 ◆

The Heart Is the Teacher, Leonard Covello's autobiography, was first published in 1958, two years after his retirement from forty-five years as a teacher and principal in the New York Public Schools, mostly in East Harlem where he lived for most of his life. Currently out of print, Covello's story should be brought back into the educational discourse, not only for its social content related to the education of immigrant students and inspiring educational stance regarding the diverse cultures and social dilemmas of East Harlem but as a reminder that our work as educators is not without a history; that many of the problems we currently struggle with were faced by others before us, sometimes confronted differently, oftentimes more intelligently. Maintaining better connections with this history, making it part of our ongoing reflection about teaching, learning, and schools, keeps the dignity of teaching and its broader social context within our gaze, providing us with larger sets of possibilities for our practice, leading us to a more discriminating stance about what is often put forward as reform.

1

I was first introduced to Leonard Covello's autobiography in 1969. In retrospect, I wonder why it took so long for me to hear about and read *The Heart Is the Teacher*. After all, I had, by then, been teaching for thirteen years and considered myself a serious student of teaching. Needless to say, perhaps, I was captivated immediately by the account, seeing in it a remarkable educator who comprehended well his East Harlem immigrant-migrant setting; articulated clearly a set of humane, inspiring purposes for himself, his students, the schools, and those in the surrounding community; and exemplified in practice a large array of educational understandings that seemed so logical, so commonsensical, so right. I was attracted as well by the basic metaphors, especially the idea of teaching emanating from the heart, an antidote, it seemed, to the way teaching was (and still is) being described in the research literature. In a very large way, "Pop," as Covello was called by many of his students, affirmed much of what I understood teaching to be—essentially a moral and intellectual endeavor. Many of my colleagues at that time thought teachers needed to remain distant, involved exclusively with the content of their subject matters. My experience, as a student and as a teacher, was filled with other messages—that personal relationships and caring mattered, that the lives of the students, in and out of school, were never really apart from whatever was being studied. I was also drawn to Covello's work because he was Italian, a person who had struggled with the immigrant experience, something I understood well as the son of Italian immigrants. It was natural to see in Covello's life and work some of my own.

Covello set the stage for his autobiographical story early, asking us to look with him out of his office window, across East River Drive to the glistening waters of the East River. It is his last day of work at the Benjamin Franklin Community High School—the center of his life for the previous twenty-two years, a period he calls his most fruitful, when he was able to do the work on behalf of young men he most wanted to do, in a part of New York City "which was looked upon by many people as a pariah community" (p. 184). But that particular view of the world is quickly replaced by a four-year-old Leonardo in Avigliano, in the south of Italy, looking out yet another window in the direction his father took when he departed in 1891 for America, then seen as the new Canaan, a land of "gold-paved streets" and "opportunity for all." He recalls his mother calling, "Narduccio, come away from the window. Your father is gone now. We must wait . . . until he calls for us and we can go to him in America" (p. 3). The window is a metaphor for the world, for the wonder of "what is to come next?"

Covello's story, including the waiting at the window, and finally the voyage to America, is an ever-repeating story told by millions of other Southern Italians who left their small towns and villages, disillusioned with their lives, their possibilities, having come to acknowledge the extreme poverty that surrounded them, believing that everything would change for the better. Close to five million Italians made the journey between 1880 and 1924. (In all, 25 million new immigrants entered the United States over this forty-four-year period.) While the Italian story is unique in many ways, it has close connections to the experience of many other "new" immigrants of that time—Eastern European Jews, Poles, Greeks—and to the more recent migration from Puerto Rico, the Dominican Republic, Central and South America, Mexico, Korea, China, and Southeast Asia. It also has many connections to the post-1920 period of African American migration from the rural south to various northern urban centers. So many of us are part of this ever-repeating story.

Since first reading Covello's autobiography, I have found myself returning to it often—especially in recent years as immigration has begun to reach levels similar to those at the turn of the century, as language concerns have reemerged in a large way, as race matters have grown more complex, and as our urban communities have begun to assume again many of the physical conditions written about so graphically at the turn of the century by Jacob Riis, among others. There was considerable hopelessness, a feeling of despair, among large numbers of early twentieth century immigrants crowded together in broken-down urban tenements, facing enormous ridicule whenever they ventured far from their ghettoized environments, having to deal with what they perceived to be a loss of their children to an unrelenting Americanization process. It was not the life they expected.

Much has changed for immigrant populations as we reach yet another century, but so much is also the same. The more recent immigrant populations who currently inhabit our deteriorating urban settings feel much of the despair that Covello describes. They, too, are as worried about their children, wondering if America's promise will ever be large enough, generous enough, inclusive enough. And African Americans, with a history as long in this country as the earliest European settlers, still find themselves far short of America's promise, served poorly in a majority of the schools and the marketplace. Covello's story is in many regards a contemporary story.

The words quoted at the beginning of my essay grace the foundation of the Statue of Liberty. From all accounts, Emma Lazarus' reading of "The New Colossus" at the Statue of Liberty dedication ceremony in 1886 generated little enthusiasm. It is possible that Lazarus had a better understanding of what the statue symbolized than most who were present at the dedication. Early in the twentieth century there was a growing resentment of the "huddled masses," "the homeless." Immigration policy changed in 1924, virtually closing the doors on those from Southern and Eastern Europe. In 1965, the United States once again changed its immigration law and reached back to the ideals expressed in "The New Colossus." But after several decades of large-scale immigration, bringing to American society a host of new cultures and energy, the public seems again ready to turn its back on those words of hope. Possibly, Covello's story will help us reach again to a more constructive response.

As I enter *The Heart Is the Teacher* as a reader, I am easily able to find myself as one of Covello's students, living in many of the same two worlds, challenging with him the social and economic circumstances of American society. As in other books I re-read, I find in Covello's story new things to think about with each reading. In my most recent encounters, for example, I have found myself more engaged with his discussions of curriculum—especially in relation to building social capacity, what is often called today a sense of empowerment, in students and community members, and of the development of intercultural understandings. I am also now more conscious of Covello's single-mindedness about the importance of community, that sense of collective caring, of solidarity. These are particularly important matters for contemporary schools, struggling as they are with the diversity of their students and related communities, trying desperately to build among their students solid commitments to powerful learning.

This book, my interaction with and around Covello's autobiographical text, is meant to bring to larger public attention a set of educational ideas that are at once enduring and possibly revolutionary, that might render to our educational discourse more energy, urgency, and challenge, providing us in the process with more ways of thinking about our schools as we go forward into yet another century.

My account cannot help but have many autobiographical qualities that will stand alongside Covello's story. Autobiography evokes, it seems, more autobiography. Stephen Spender writes in this regard: "In literature the autobiographical is transferred. It is no longer the writer's experience: it becomes everyone's. The autobiographer is no longer writing about himself: he is writing about life" (quoted in Jerome Buckley, 1986, p. 44). Covello wrote from an educator's heart; he told a teacher's story. In that sense, because I am a teacher, it is also my story, necessarily evoking some of my experience.

❖ 2 ❖

For Italian immigrants and their families, Covello's story has great resonance. I can easily see in him many other Italians, even my father. I also know, however, that his story has unique qualities, as does my father's immigrant story, as does every immigrant story, regardless of national origin.

Each decision to leave one's "paese," the village of one's family, carried a *particular* set of hopes and fears, a range of personal expressions. The Ellis Island experience was seen in millions of ways, told differently, it seems, by each immigrant. Once here the story also assumed many different patterns. The East Harlem experience was not exactly the Cleveland or Chicago experience. For that matter, life on Mulberry Street in New York was not a mirror of life on East 112th Street. The Italian settlements in the Upper Peninsula of Michigan were very different from those in the hills beyond San Francisco. Calling attention to the differences is not to deny the large array of commonalities, but the commonalities should not mask the personal stories that have given meaning to many individuals and families. There is still a tendency to lump stories together as we speak of the more recent immigrants, as if there is nothing undifferentiated about them. Is the Chinese experience in America the Korean experience? the Philippine experience? the Japanese experience? Is there a difference between immigrants from Chiapas and those from Guadalajara in Mexico? Do they have different stories to tell? Clearly they do, but it seems easier to generalize, to stay at arm's length, not get so involved that the differences and the resulting complexities stand out.

The most similar patterns of my personal immigrant family story may reside more in Italy than in the United States. I share this family story early in this text to establish a personal context. While it may appear sentimental, my purpose is not sentimental. I believe, for example, that the story is more common than unusual, possibly helping us as teachers to think differently about those we meet who appear to be living a different life from the one we have known or are currently living. It might also encourage more autobiographical reflection, something all of us as teachers need to engage in more fully.

My father, Giuseppe Perrone, was born in 1887, the same year as Covello, in Ribera, in the province of Agrigento, Sicily. As the only child of an invalid mother and a father who died when he was three, he was in the wheat fields at the age of five, working, providing some of what he and his mother needed for survival. That hard working life, which my father shared with most others of his generation in Sicily, persisted for virtually all of his years.

As was the case for most poor boys in his community, schooling was absent, in spite of a three-year "compulsory" education law that was then in place. He grew up illiterate in the Italian language, which was the common circumstance for Southern Italians of his era. Illiteracy rates were, for example, as high as 90% for much of the nineteenth century; they were still over 70% in 1905. The dramatic change in literacy rates in Southern Italy occurred after the First World War.

Growing up illiterate did not mean that my father was without a sense of culture. He was familiar with the music of his region and he had a great love for the opera. He knew by heart many of the arias. He also knew the names of many Italian painters and could identify their works. My older siblings remember well being entertained by my father's singing and acting out of various arias. And he often took them to museums so they could see the works of "all the Italian painters and sculptors." I can't say if his knowledge and interests were common—though I expect he would have said that was the case.

In 1909, at the age of twenty-two, my father was married to Anna D'Anna, the eldest of several children, at the time sixteen years of age. As was customary, the marriage had been arranged by their parents. In contrast to most children in Ribera, certainly in relation to females, my mother was very well educated for her time. She had gone to school for eight years and was an active reader and writer, a scribe for most people in her community, identified as "*la professora.*"

In 1910, soon after the birth of my eldest sister, Leonarda, my father made the journey to the United States, to the "new world of opportunity." Like Covello's father, he also left a family to peer from the window, toward the West, wondering when and if a reunion would occur. Within the mythology of Italian immigration, going to America was the aim of *all* young men. Yet, in fact, only a small number actually went. Somehow, that part of the story is seldom recounted. And among those who made the journey, large numbers returned, especially in the initial decades.

After five months in the tenements of East Harlem, my father took a job with the New York Central Railroad (NYCRR), working on the rail line from Chicago into central Iowa. He says that moving away from New York City was important to him, a means of establishing greater independence, where his individual character would matter. He spoke of New York as a sea of disrespected, heavily exploited people. After two and a half years in Iowa, he was assigned by the NYCRR to Bath, Michigan, a small community some fifteen miles from Lansing, the state capital. He was, in this town, the only recent immigrant, the only person with southern European roots, and the only Catholic. He stood out in every way. Along with his sociability, always his hallmark, his reputation for hard work and ingenuity at problem solving earned him considerable respect. Townspeople saw him as a "model immigrant," everything immigration was supposed to produce. All accounts of him in the published histories of Bath describe him as "the popular Italian immigrant."

While he was by 1914 in a position to bring his family to the United States, World War I intervened. He and my mother thought it would be better and safer to wait out the war years. In 1917 my father was drafted, finding himself part of the American Expeditionary Force in the trenches of France. Having never gone beyond Agrigento in his early life, he found himself very quickly a "world traveler." He distinguished himself at the Battles of Saint-Mihiel and the Marne, among the decisive engagements of the war, and returned to Bath as a well-decorated war veteran.

It was two more years (1921) before my mother and sister, now almost eleven, passed through Ellis Island and moved on to Bath, Michigan. My mother was not eager to leave Ribera or her family. It was exclusively a matter of duty. I can imagine the long train ride from New York—some twenty-three hours. It must have made the cross-Atlantic voyage seem, in many respects, short. Bath was clearly a disappointing sight. Most of the roads in the area were gravel and dust. Moreover, electrification, which had reached Ribera in 1918, was still several years away. There was no one to talk with beyond her husband and daughter. Shopping was a nightmare. Nothing seemed familiar and the shopkeepers were not particularly helpful. Even worse, the church across the street from her home was Protestant, something she knew nothing about. Who in Ribera had ever heard of a Baptist?

When Leonarda was brought to the local elementary school, after having attended school in Ribera for five years, she was placed with six-year-olds "because she didn't speak English." This was not an untypical response by schools across the United States. The belief was that it would be easier to learn English in a setting where children's use of English was at a basic stage. My mother was outraged and lost all respect for the school. She spent almost no time thereafter in any school, for any reason. This was not her place, her country, her desired life.

Three more children soon entered the family—in 1922, 1923, and 1925. It was through these initial four children that my father's personal history of learning to read and write English took form. Given his social character, he wanted to be able to read the newspapers, to converse with his neighbors about events in the world. My sisters especially remember reading with him, teaching him words he didn't recognize, answering his ongoing questions—"what does this mean?" While illiterate in Italian, he became fully literate in English, a consumer of newspapers and magazines, able to write more easily, as the years passed, the daily reports his work called for. And, being outside an Italian-speaking environment for several years, certainly from 1913 to 1921, his spoken English was well advanced.

The conflicts that were so endemic in Covello's East Harlem and in the various "Little Italys" across the country around education and work were not present in our household. My father had fully embraced the view that education mattered—that work could wait. In this regard, his Americanization came early. My older siblings remember well his ongoing admonition—"read, read." He brought home books and magazines given to him by others and he took the children to the library often so they could check out books. He didn't stay in touch with what was being read—that didn't really matter. As one of my sisters recalls, he was most content when everyone was reading, and I don't think it had anything to do with quiet.

When my closest-in-age brother and I were born, in 1931 and 1933, respectively, and growing up, the educational patterns had been set. We were expected to do well in school, as the other four had done well in school. My mother's view was that doing well in school was nothing really special. What that really meant was that she wasn't much impressed with "Americans" and their talents. Americans, for her, were all those who weren't Italian.

When Bath was no longer a center of railroad maintenance, my father's job was moved to Lansing, an urban setting. This meant more responsibility, a larger maintenance crew to take care of, and lengthier reports to complete each evening. The move to Lansing in 1940 was undoubtedly a large relief for my mother, as Lansing had an Italian community, Catholic churches, and import stores with more recognizable cheeses, pastas, olives, and condiments. It meant for her a more social life. Even *Il Progresso*, an Italian newspaper from New York, was readily available.

When we moved to Lansing, I was then entering the third grade, my next brother, the fifth, my closest sister, the tenth. My eldest sister was by then married, my eldest brother was in college, and the next brother stayed in Bath to complete his last year of high school. Without him, the football, basketball, and baseball teams would have been without their best player and the music program would have been without its only baritone player. My father thought it was appropriate for him to stay in Bath. My mother thought it was decidedly unnatural—another sign that she should never have come to this country.

Lansing was the setting in which Italianness became more prominent for me. I heard "dago" and "wop" for the first time. I suspect the larger Italian presence was a factor. In Bath the smells and sounds of my mother's kitchen were distinctive, never duplicated. In Lansing the smells and sounds were more present beyond our home. The Cangemi family, whose yard adjoined ours, my parents' *comare* and *compare*, became fully intertwined with our lives. The only other Vito I knew growing up was in the Cangemi household. It was as close as we would ever be to Italian village life.

Other than my eldest sister, whose marriage had been arranged, none of the children married Italians. This was very sad for my mother, who believed for most of her life that marriages should be arranged and Italians should marry Italians. And marriages were, in fact, still being arranged at the time I was growing up. My second sister, Rose, still recounts my mother's arrangements for her marriage. She appealed to my father, who agreed that she didn't have to be a part of any arranged marriage. He went to my mother to tell her that Rose did not want to be married in the "Italian way" and would find her own husband. All discussions about arranged marriage ended.

My father enjoyed playing cards and was very skilled. We played cards together a great deal, mostly bidding games that were like euchre. But he took easily to bridge when my brother came back from World War II as a bridge player. And while he was a skilled boccie ball player, he thought American baseball was far more interesting. A baseball game would always take precedence over boccie.

It was striking for us (the children in the family) to observe the differences in our lives when we visited relatives in New York and New Jersey. Most of the children we met—especially those older than fourteen—seemed to have little connection to school. Work was a more central aspect of their life stories. While we were interested in libraries, museums, and baseball, they found greater amusement in the life on the streets. "Hanging out" had a different meaning for them. These visits were clearly made for my mother, who could easily have settled into these fully Italian communities. My father, though, couldn't wait to get away, back to his home in Michigan.

I have often thought about those I met in these big urban Italian communities. If my father had decided to stay in New York, would my brothers, sisters, and I have completed school? Moreover, knowing more about the "old country," as I now do, what if my father had not decided to make the journey across the Atlantic? Would I have found my way into the wheat fields, laboring in the olive groves, living fully the poor Southern Italian life my father was living before he left? There is a point when virtually all immigrant children think about such things. It keeps us asking who we are and whether we should be different than we are. It also makes us more conscious of the power of the choices our families have made, rooting us intimately in the great drama of human migration.

I got closer to the Italian story in 1955 when my father asked me to sign, as a witness, a legal document transferring a house and a small parcel of land to relatives in Ribera. Various relatives had lived in that house over the years my mother had been gone. I knew that my parents had sent money to family members in Ribera for many years, certainly into the early post–World War II period, but I didn't know about the property. When I remarked that I didn't know my parents had a house and land and suggested that I might have been interested in the property, my father expressed great surprise. "Why," he exclaimed, "would you have any interest in a property in Italy? You are an American!" As I told him, the act of signing the paper seemed like a final break with the old country. My mother cried. As she said then, and often thereafter, "I wish I had never come to this country." I think about my mother a lot. America was not much of a "Promised Land" for her.

What stands out for me as I think about my mother was her fierce pride in her cultural base. She could read English but she preferred the Italian newspapers and magazines. She spoke English, in her own way perhaps, outside the home, when she had to, but she seldom spoke English at home. I remember asking her to *please* speak English to my friends who came over to the house. Most of the time, she wouldn't. I was asking too much. I have since come to appreciate her stance. She could have spoken English but she clearly didn't want to. My mother's stance regarding using her native language in her own home is understandable, a means of preserving her dignity, her sense of efficacy. I hear often today from teachers that their students' mothers insist on speaking their native languages in the home and "how damaging this is for their children." It isn't damaging!

Though restrained in her enthusiasm for those outside the family, or not Italian, my mother would nonetheless bring food to those who were sick, always ready to give to those in need. She was, in times of stress for others, a particularly generous person.

My father was very accepting of others, regardless of their cultural or racial backgrounds. He always had an ease about him. He also remembered his beginnings. When I was in high school, the new workers on the track crews were mainly Mexican immigrants. That they didn't speak English reminded my father of his early years without any ability to use English. He spoke of the Mexicans as the "new Italians." And he asked me to come to work with him on several occasions to help the new workers complete various work forms "since you are studying Spanish in school." I was impressed that he was conscious of my Spanish language coursework, since what I was studying in school was never a topic of discussion.

The story of my parents, our family, is not a story our children know well. They have heard many times all the accounts, but it is difficult for them to imagine their authenticity. Who works in the fields at age five? How could anyone grow up illiterate? Yet for me it remains an inspiring story. It keeps me sympathetic in relation to the other, the person with the different experience, living between cultures. It keeps before me an ongoing concern about racial and economic justice. It also keeps alive the sense of possibility. Leonard Covello made his background an essential ingredient of his work, the way he thought about the other. I understand that stance.

❖ 3 ❖

Leonard Covello came to the United States in 1896 with his mother and two younger brothers. His father had made the journey five years earlier. It was hardly a joyous time, leaving grandparents, uncles, aunts, and cousins behind in Avigliano. While everyone spoke of "how wonderful life would be in America," they also knew that life in America was not paradise, that in many ways it was filled with more difficulties than Avigliano.

Ellis Island, now a memorial to America's European immigrant history, was to the Covellos a nightmare of lines, guards, and uncertainty, a place where the Covello children were occasionally separated from their mother. Covello writes of the first instance: "When we ran back to her, she clutched us convulsively . . . in her eyes there was the disbelieving look of a mother who never expected to see her children again" (p. 20).

The family's first home was in a tenement flat on 112th Street, near the East River, now the site of Jefferson Park. There were others from Avigliano close by, the people Covello's father said "you could always count on." Village understandings lived long for Southern Italians as they do now for immigrants from Mexico or Cambodia. While such understandings may seem to establish boundaries, they are understandable, even necessary.

Once he was taken to school by his father, his father never again entered a school. His mother never stepped foot in a New York City school. The separation from this American institution was large. Those who helped Covello understand what was going on were other Italian children from Avigliano who had been in the country for several years. In the old country, parents and adult family members were the principal interpreters of the world. They possessed real authority. Here in America, children became the interpreters, the "go-betweens." I am not sure that we understand or appreciate clearly enough the role immigrant children play in their families' socialization. Imagine the responsibility these children bear, the knowledge they come to possess. If we began in our schools with such an understanding, the language of deficits that currently dominates so much of the discourse around recent immigrant children might fade away. Additionally, it is difficult not to think of *all* students in the schools as potentially productive translators of cultures, of various subject matters. Building more of their schooling around this translator role would give far greater meaning to their schooling. It would comprise another effort toward empowerment and self-efficacy.

The biggest surprise for Covello in these American schools was the female teachers that he encountered. In Italy, all the schoolmasters Covello had seen were men and their discipline was firm and "stinging." He soon found that his female teachers, with their short bamboo switches, could be just as frightening. The difference was, as he suggests, that they often apologized for being too firm.

The family name was actually Coviello and not Covello. It became Covello because one of Leonard's elementary teachers changed it. She thought the *i* got in the way and it was hard to pronounce the *ie* after *v* and before *l*. His father was very upset. As he noted to his son, "From Leonardo to Leonard I can follow . . . but you don't change a family name." Covello noted, "What difference does it make? . . . It's more American. The *i* doesn't help anything." His friend Vito Accurso, who was present for this exchange, concurred that names in America often changed. As he said, he wasn't called Vito at school. His teachers had changed the name to Victor. Leonard's mother told him he must tell his teacher that the *i* had to go back into his name: "A person's life and his honor is in his name. He never changes it. A name is not a shirt or a piece of underwear." Leonard could only say "you don't understand. It was not a mistake. The *i* is out." Leonard's mother heard over and over again, for the rest of her years, "you just don't understand." She often said to her son in exasperation, "you understand everything, I understand nothing!" She must have wondered, "What kind of country is this?" (pp. 29–31).

Leonard Covello's story could probably be told by countless others. Parents felt disenfranchised. Children were struggling between two sets of cultural values. Schools at the time, however, did not make this conflict their concern. It was a sign of their detachment from what truly mattered for immigrant families.

While it is possible to say that such alterations of a name wouldn't happen today, and I often hear such sentiments, I know that large numbers of recent immigrants are going through experiences with many similarities. How many Hispanic, Asian, Haitian, African, and Middle Eastern children are asked to respond to names they know would be unfamiliar to their parents? Clearly, given our linguistic experience, we may have trouble pronouncing some names, *but* we can learn to do so and we should.

I can recall a classroom I visited where a child whose name was Jésus was called Jessie by the teacher. When the teacher was asked why she didn't call him Jésus (hay-SUS in phonetic terms), she said "I couldn't call him Jésus (JEE-sus in phonetic terms)." Because the teacher called him Jessie, other children called him Jessie. He *became* Jessie. More recently, one of my Chinese students introduced herself as Nancy, the name she was given in school because Yin Mui was just "too difficult" for her teachers to pronounce. Does any of this matter? Of course, it matters.

In a culture such as ours, in which American identity is often defined narrowly, students do, on occasion, come to feel ashamed of their names or see liabilities resulting from their names, essentially what they understand to be basic discrimination. Covello described an experience that may not be uncommon, even in our own day. It depicts well, I believe, the dilemmas of being a "foreigner."

While walking to school I was stopped by a student, Jésus Morales, who had graduated just the term before. He was Puerto Rican, but he could have been Italian or Jewish or almost anything at all. . . . "Pop," Morales explained, . . . "a man should never be ashamed of his nationality, but I can't help it. I gotta change my name."

Here was the name-changing routine all over again. How many times had I heard it during the course of my life! Each succeeding wave of immigrants seeking to lose their identity, seeking to lose themselves in a nothingness, a characterless void in which one human being was exactly like the other. . . .

Morales told me about the jobs he thought he had lost because of his Puerto Rican origin. But he was never really quite sure until he applied for work in an office. It was a good job and the office manager was about to hire him until he heard the name. "Morales! That's Puerto Rican. I can't hire Puerto Ricans here."

The office manager was firm. "Change your name, that's all I can say."

"So you see," Morales added, "that's how it is. I've got to change my name if I wanna get a job."

He was right, in a way. Just the simple business of dropping a few letters from a name and the world might become another place. But would it, really? "You could get away with it, Morales," I said. "No question. You don't have the trace of a Spanish accent. Who'd know the difference?"

The youth nodded.

"The only trouble is *you* would know the difference. Your mother and father would know, as well as all of your friends and the people who have been around you since you were born. That's the trouble." (pp. 224–225)

Covello understood the pressures his students faced. He knew that American society wasn't always fair, didn't provide to all people a full measure of justice. Unlike most of his teaching colleagues, however, he wasn't silent about the circumstances that surrounded him. He didn't tell his students that "hard work" was all it took in America. He knew better. And his students knew better. If it was only hard work, most of their parents would be living in luxury. They worked very hard at jobs most native-born Americans wouldn't do, and they were struggling to survive. He also didn't tell his students that this was a discrimination-free country, filled with "justice for all." Again, he knew better. The evidence was everywhere—people of color, immigrants, those who were poor, just didn't matter enough in this society. Have things changed? In relation to this issue, the Central Park East Secondary School used as its central curriculum question for a recent year, "Whose America is it?" It was a means for students and teachers to explore longstanding immigrant, African American, Native American issues. It also helped students to understand more fully the distribution of power in American society.

Covello tells another story in his autobiography that relates to the foregoing, while raising yet another important point. As Covello's students went off to the army in 1917, heeding President Wilson's call to patriotism and "the war to end all wars," Covello felt he should also go, primarily as a show of support for his students. He ended up in basic training with many of them. He noted in regard to one of his former students, whom he respected greatly, how he insisted on doing everything in basic training better than all others, often pushing himself to exhaustion. Covello remembers asking him why he had to be first in everything. "Do you feel," Covello inquired, "that it would have been different had you been raised in Italy instead of America? Would the compulsion to win have been less?" The young man replied, "I am sure of it. It is maybe because I was born in Sicily and still do not speak like an American that I have to show that I am good for more than hanging around street corners. It is something as childish as this" (p. 118).

Those who are different in America are often made to feel that they have to be twice as good, work twice as hard. African Americans have long felt burdened in this way. No one should be put in this position. The need for moving beyond surface appearances, to understand that every human person has unique capacities and a need to be shown respect, is large. We can learn to see in others ourselves. I think here of a poem by a young Boston-area student from Cambodia, which closes as follows:

> What is it like when you walk in
>   the street and everybody turns around
>   to look at you and you don't know
>   that they are looking at you?
> Then, when you find out, you want to
>   hide your face but you don't know
>   where to hide because they are
>   everywhere.
> You have to live in somebody else's country to
>   understand.
>   (Noy Chou, in Denzer & Wheelock, 1990, p. 84)

But it is not "somebody else's country." It is Noy Chou's country as it is my country and your country, We need to stand together, to see ourselves and our possibilities as connected. This is a lesson we must teach well in our schools.

As Covello thought of his own education, struggling to speak English, always worried about mispronunciations, feeling ridicule from his "American" classmates, he also remembered many of his Italian classmates who saw the school as a prison, who left school at age twelve to work full-time in support of their families. The truant officers, he noted, were "happy about it," fewer children to worry about. Even as I know that the truant officers were, at this time, over-burdened, it seems also clear that the Italian children weren't important enough to follow up on seriously.

I work in many schools today where absence rates are particularly high—25%–35% on a daily basis. The attitude is much the same as Covello describes. I have often heard such statements as "The school functions better without them." "What would we do if everyone on our rolls actually came to school?" "*Those* kids don't want to learn. They are not worth worrying about." Who are the students who aren't worth worrying about? Those who are poor, darker skinned, African American, Hispanic, often newly arrived immigrants. I have conversed with many alienated students who believe most adults in their schools are hostile toward them, wishing they would just stay away. They do not feel wanted. We are not really so far removed today from what Covello described.

❖ **4** ❖

Covello mastered the tasks of elementary school, memorizing words and places, completing the various worksheet assignments, though understanding that all the different aspects of his life—in school, in the streets, within the family, in church—were disconnected. With life at P.S. 83 behind him, Covello went off in 1903 to Morris High School, assigned to a set of courses he had no choice about. About his assignment to German language, he notes: "Who put it there I never knew" (p. 43).

Morris was coeducational. This was different for Covello, and it especially posed problems for the Italian boys, who understood that girls were to be kept apart. It meant another adjustment. A larger difference, however, was all the non-Italian students, who seemed to Covello to be better off, were well dressed, had money, and seemed self-assured, with a social life that did not include new immigrants. Being a distinctive "minority" in this setting kept the fear of ridicule constant.

Covello was, of course, correct in his assessment of the high school as heavily middle class and non-foreign. Few students from lower socioeconomic class backgrounds found their way beyond grade eight. The Italian population would have been very small. The secondary schools did not assume a more universal character—places that most students in the age cohort actually attended—until the 1920s. And it was 1950 before the majority—over half—of students actually graduated from high school.

Even as high schools are more universal today, they still tend to be stratified by race and class. At one level, geography, where people live, keeps social classes apart. Geography also contributes to considerable racial isolation in our schools. In urban settings, students of color and those who are economically poor now dominate the schools. Beyond the cities, the schools are more middle class and white. In settings where there are higher levels of integration of students around race and class, tracking systems—the separation of students by perceptions of ability, gift, or talent—tend to exist, which most often result in keeping racial and class separations intact. Our schools are not yet as democratic as they need to be, and the resources are not distributed in ways that assure high levels of academic support for all students. Those of us who teach must keep raising questions about the inequities. Why must the struggle for better schools be the burden primarily of the students and their parents?

What most impressed Covello about his teachers was that they didn't live in the neighborhood near the school, dressed better than and spoke differently from his neighbors. They seemed, he suggested, "to come from somewhere beyond the horizon" (p. 47), from an outer world, an American world, a place where people lived better and had an easier time. "But in trying to make a good impression on our teachers," something Covello and his fellow Italian immigrants felt they had to do, he remembers, "it was always at the expense of our family and what was Italian in us" (p. 47). In most settings today, things are not much different. In our urban centers, teachers tend to live far away from the schools they teach in. I have been in many urban settings in which teachers make it clear they would *never* send their own children to the schools they teach in. Their students know their sentiments. Can this bring confidence? But circumstances could be different. As a means of addressing racial and cultural concerns, there is a growing tradition in Native American communities to bring elders into the schools, persons who share community stories, help keep native languages and cultural stories alive, assure that children have persons with whom to make personal connections. Non–Native American teachers in these settings comment on how much more talkative the children are. They see major differences in their energy and interest in school. In such settings, and the possibilities go beyond Native American schools, children can be more themselves; they don't have to turn their backs on their families or their traditions. This should be the situation for all children.

There once was a tradition of teachers making home visits as a means of making more personal connections with their students' families and home situations. In the process, teachers also became better known. Such a practice should be revived. It is also clearly possible for teachers to learn about the languages, cultures, and neighborhoods of their students, to make those languages, cultures, and neighborhoods more central to life in the classrooms. This is all a matter of respect, of genuine reciprocity.

At the end of eleventh grade, following in the footsteps of the majority of Italian students at that time, Covello left school to work full time, believing he could make a larger contribution to his family's well-being, making life easier. His mother's failing health and mounting medical expenses "were more than I could bear," he wrote. There were no questions from the family when he announced that he had left school. He was certainly old enough to work. But what of the school? What kind of guidance did he receive there? As he writes: "What stands foremost in my mind concerning the decision was the indifference and lack of guidance at the high school itself. I simply turned in my books . . . and went away. No one spoke to me. No one asked me why I was leaving" (p. 52).

Many students drop out of school today because no one in the school seems to have noticed that they were ever there. What if Covello had been a middle-class "American" student? Would he have departed so easily, so unnoticeably? In response to the question of another Italian student, already out of school, who asked if the principal said anything to him, Covello noted: "Did you expect the principal was going to come out and kiss me? He doesn't even know I'm alive. Nobody knows we're alive inside there [and he meant here the Italian students], except maybe one or two teachers. They don't even know when you come and when you go" (p. 53). I meet many young people with similar views. Why do we tolerate this level of indifference, of disrespect?

One of the dilemmas at Covello's school, even beyond his Italian background, was the size of the school—over 3,000 students were enrolled. Who could really keep track of the students? Students need to be well known to be educated well. This implies small schools or small learning communities within larger schools. Schools that work best for immigrant children, for students of color, for those who are poor, are, in fact, *small* schools (Cotton, 1997). In such settings, personal attention is more possible; the use of outside resources—including opportunities for service, apprenticeships, and college courses—is simpler to organize and sustain; parents, guardians, and community people find such schools easier to enter, to play a role in; teachers find it easier in such settings to talk with one another, to assure a more connected, relevant curriculum. In these small schools, students are less likely to drop out because they *are* well known. In many of our urban communities, these understandings are beginning to take hold. New York City and Chicago, in particular, have devoted considerable energy to the organization of small schools. Doing something about the size and scale of schools is a reform direction with good potential. Yet the major reform directions are more about standardizing the curriculum and promoting high-stakes tests.

What Covello learned when he left school to become a full-time worker was that the compensation was not great enough to make a substantial difference in family circumstances. Moreover, he was not particularly happy and he stayed mostly at home when not working, burying himself in books. His childhood friend whom he later married, Mary Accurso, convinced Covello that he should go back to school, that conditions might not be good for his family but the family would survive as it had been surviving. His parents offered no rejoinder to his decision to return to school as they had given no protest about his decision to leave school. Southern Italian immigrant children often had to make their own decisions about such things. In saying this, I am immediately brought back to my own teaching experience, hearing many of my teacher colleagues speak about how irresponsible so many of their students are. Yet many of these students, like Covello, were regularly making major decisions about their lives, often without much adult support. We need to make connections to that particular level of genuine responsibility.

Were there benefits from his year of full-time work? Covello says that being out in the work world meant meeting many different people from many different nationalities. He began to think differently about the Irish, the Poles, the Jews. "I found out," he says, "that New York did not consist of merely Americans and Italians, but rather of people in varying stages of the thing called Americanization. . . . I began to find myself reacting differently toward the bustling humanity around me" (p. 56).

Work was for Covello an important means of crossing boundaries, of moving beyond the isolation of Avigliano and his East Harlem neighborhood. How, today, do we help students get beyond the boundaries that exist for them? We speak of the immigrant ghettos of Covello's growing-up period as if such insular islands no longer exist. Housing patterns, dictated to a large degree by social attitudes and economic status, still leave most people in ghettoized situations. Those who live in the middle- and upper-class suburban communities of America see few people different from themselves. They don't see much of the growing population of color in the United States. While they have larger horizons than their poorer neighbors in America's central cities, they still travel fairly circumscribed routes. And African Americans, Southeast Asians, and Hispanics live out much of their lives in relatively familiar settings. Students in many of our urban communities seldom go outside of narrowly drawn geographical boundaries in which most people look like them and dress like them.

We need to find ways of supporting students to move beyond their physical and cultural boundaries, to meet, work with, get to know others better. Work often makes this more possible. Can work become more connected to the schools? more integral to the curriculum? We now have increasing numbers of schools, mostly in urban settings, developing school-to-work, -career, -postsecondary-education programs. They should be broader, involve more students, be related to richer and more diverse work/career settings. Some of what Covello found outside of school regarding learning about others could be more connected to school.

A particular concern of many contemporary secondary schools remains students who work while in school. One difference is that work doesn't necessarily lead students out of school permanently—as was often the case in earlier times. As it is, close to 70% of secondary school students are employed, working on average from fifteen to eighteen hours per week, principally in the burgeoning fast-food and service industries. Rather than viewing this work as positive, contributing to student responsibility and a sense of usefulness, however, those in schools speak of it primarily as lessening student commitments to the school's academic and extracurricular programs and fostering what they believe to be an unhealthy materialism. Once again it is as if the work of the school and the larger world must be in conflict, that there aren't connecting points of consequence that actually affect the students and their learning.

While I acknowledge that students who work over twenty hours a week (and this encompasses almost half of student workers) tend to suffer academically within the *current* structure of schools (time-bound, restrictive in terms of the number of courses a student must take each semester, and curricularly insular), the work of students needs to be thought about more constructively (as does the structure of schools). Students, for example, speak of what they do in their work as "being useful," "creating a sense of independence" and "responsibility." They also tend to enjoy their work. And employers see them as reliable and competent (Perrone et al., 1981). Are such perspectives to be negated? Is there no way to use such awareness?

I often ask teachers why they don't have students maintain journals of their work experiences; why they don't make these work experiences the focus of study in courses in health, nutrition, science, economics, mathematics, government, history, and literature; why they don't engage more directly the materialist culture that is so potent in American society and contributes heavily to student employment. Can't the world these students have entered into so fully be connected to the ongoing and important work of the schools?

A number of schools have actually sought means of constructing more productive school–work connections. In some cases, this has been done through work-site internships or apprenticeships. Students in the Children's Hospital collaborative, one of the work-site programs of the Fenway School in Boston, carry out as part of their work a research project under the supervision of a hospital staff person that is the primary science-related project required by the school. Students in the Elementary School Teaching Program associated with the Cambridge Rindge & Latin School write children's books as part of their English requirement. At Central Park East, students must complete an internship/work requirement for graduation that includes a reflective paper placing the work in historical/cultural context. And in several of the schools associated with the Annenberg Rural Challenge, teachers and students are actively engaged together in entrepreneurial enterprises in their communities. Creating businesses, run by students, has become a well-integrated element of the academic program. The rationale in these settings for encouraging entrepreneurial activities is that students need to learn how to create work so they can live where they wish to live. These are certainly beginning efforts—road maps to an even larger set of possibilities.

More confident, more comfortable with students from other backgrounds after a year out of school, Covello became, when he returned, more involved in school activities and more engaged with the academic course work. He was also more engaged by matters of social injustice, something he thought about a good deal while outside of school. He notes, though, that he was cautioned *not* to speak or write about such things. He wondered why "the oppression of people"—whether peasants in Russia treated cruelly by the Czarist government or "immigrants and Negroes" in the United States who faced injustice everyday—wasn't a topic for the school. How much has changed? Is the school a major venue for intensively examining critical social issues?

Why is it so hard in our schools to actually examine the conditions that exist for our students and their families? for those who are described as different? One of the most important contemporary stories in Boston's history relates to the court-ordered desegregation of the schools. In many schools, teachers are admonished *not* to discuss it, not to present the *Eyes on the Prize* account of the violence. Race plays a particularly large role in the life of Boston. Not to make this a matter of examination seems unhealthy. Yet it goes, for the most part, unexamined.

We have a curious educational history in regard to what are considered "controversial issues." In some respects, almost everything that exists in the world has aspects that could be seen as controversial. Do we want our students to ask why hunger exists in the world? Or why there are homeless people in the streets? Or why African-Americans face such harsh discrimination? Or why there is such disparity of wealth in the United States? Or why so much money is spent on space exploration? Or why the atom bomb was actually used on a civilian population? Or how our cities can be more livable? Or how universal health care can be assured? Or how we can more effectively preserve the environment? Or what the possibilities and problems are in relation to genetic engineering? Or what the problems are with the various books that people want to censor in some form? Or what the abortion struggle is about? Or why the school restricts students' rights to expression or assembly? Or why our schools are so poorly equipped and maintained? Shouldn't school classrooms be venues for conversation about the world, places where students learn to engage critical issues thoughtfully, weighing carefully the evidence, coming to understand alternative perspectives? In relation to the foregoing, it is a delight to be in the Urban Academy, a small public school in New York City, where everything studied is presented through alternative views, a range of questions and interpretations. One interesting recent course was titled, "Don't Read That Book: Censorship in America." Another was "Who Freed the Slaves?" As one student shared with me, "I have learned to separate a person's ideas and beliefs from the person. I can now disagree with a person's ideas without feeling I must also physically attack or ridicule the person." That is an important lesson. Is there any better place than a school for that kind of learning?

I can remember well, as a young secondary school teacher, being told that *The Communist Manifesto* should not be read—that it would, in the prevailing Cold War environment, cause considerable trouble. Yet my students and I read it, came to understand the context for it, and examined the Soviet Union in relation to it. Students saw our use of the text as a measure of my respect for them, my willingness to take them seriously as thoughtful persons. Parents told me they learned much from their children. Their expectations for their children's schooling also went up.

In settings in which the world is permitted to enter the classroom, where students are encouraged to ask about the connections between what they study and what they read in the newspapers, see on television, and observe in the streets, what is often called controversial is just ongoing inquiry. This is a healthier place for teachers and students to stand.

❖ 5 ❖

Covello's experience of leaving school made a large impact on him, as he became a teacher and school principal. In the 1930s at Benjamin Franklin, the pressures on young men to leave school and support their families were especially large. Over 75% of the East Harlem population was on public assistance; life was extremely difficult. Covello made sure, though, that leaving school would still not come easily for his students. Anyone contemplating leaving or making the decision to leave had to meet personally with Covello. They knew he would push them very hard as well as be exceptionally persuasive about their need to stay in school. He was prepared to offer tutoring assistance, even some financial assistance if this was the problem. He was also willing to go to students' homes to meet with their families. He didn't keep them all. But he also had, it seems, a difficult time putting those who left out of his mind. He felt he had a responsibility to check in with them to see how they were doing.

In 1937, for example, he invited every student who had left the school prior to graduation to return for the "Old Friendship Club," to renew their ties with the school and many of the teachers, to make use of the school's services, including its libraries and adult education programs, to know that they were not forgotten (pp. 213–214). This outreach effort obviously went beyond the norm. To the surprise of many, who suggested to Covello that the "Old Friendship Club" would be a bust, large numbers of former students showed up for the initial meeting, pleased to know that the school was still there for them. Many came back to regular meetings of the club as well as other evening programs. In addition, many served actively on school-community committees. Covello was able to speak about many former school-leavers, commenting often on the fact that they were good fathers and husbands, doing good things with their lives. Benjamin Franklin wasn't just a school for those who went on to college, to the professions. All of our schools could be such community-oriented schools.

Knowing the myriad ways that Covello stayed in touch with his students over the years, the fact that he was involved in their lives, visited them in hospitals, even prisons, people occasionally asked him: Don't you "get . . . tired of the boys?" Covello noted in response: "I ask them if they get tired of people they love" (p. 215). In general, teachers seem quite self-conscious about any talk of "loving the students," "loving the challenge" in meeting children and young people each day, "loving the teaching-learning exchange." Yet it is love that keeps teachers fully engaged in their work. Students often ask me, "Don't you get tired of reading all our papers?" My response over the years has been much the same. "I love the papers, they are enormously interesting, almost always challenging, filled with things for me to think more about." I loved the students I worked with in Lansing, Michigan, as a secondary school teacher. I loved their questions, their sense of humor, their language, the care they expressed toward one another, their willingness to work hard at tasks they cared about. I love, in many of the same ways, my current students at Harvard, their energy, their social commitment, their care for one another, their willingness to go beyond the norm. To gain this level of awareness of and derive this kind of joy from one's students, it is necessary to know them well, to be wide awake to their ongoing intentions, to care about the quality of the social and educational exchange.

There is a good deal of talk today about "burnout." That is supposed to be the fate of those who devote themselves, as Covello did, to their work. Most of the exceptional teachers I know, who give a high level of personal and professional intensity to their work with children and young people, don't speak of burnout. They speak of all they are learning, of the interactions that caused them to step back and reflect on some aspect of human action, of the fresh ideas that have been sparked for them, of things students taught them, of new ways of helping students gain greater control of their lives, of the rewards of their ongoing dialogic encounters. I receive calls almost daily from teachers I have worked with over many years who have a story to tell me about something a student said or wrote, how students responded to a particular event or curriculum idea, something they are considering to bring to their students. A recent story related to me was of a five-year-old child who wanted to plant some "pretty rocks" so she could grow many "new pretty rocks." I loved the story. These teachers are intellectually engaged, loving their work. They don't have the time or inclination to think about burnout. Entering teaching with this kind of disposition is, of course, helpful. It addresses the reciprocity of teaching that is so important, that sense of always being both teacher and learner.

It is such a disposition that enabled Covello to say at the conclusion of his career with the New York public schools, "I believe and will always believe in the potential of every boy to lead a good and useful life. . . . The great boys I have known . . . exist in all boys" (p. 275). Those who are fully engaged with their work see possibilities, not liabilities. They lose the language of pathology, the language of stigmatization. They have a sympathy with their students.

The foregoing sentiment comes through well at another point in Covello's life—when he went back to his boyhood home in Avigliano in 1928. He describes feeling content, fully at peace on an ancient mountain slope. What were his thoughts? "I thought about my pupils at Dewitt Clinton and wished they could have been with me to feel something of what I felt about their own people and their past" (p. 175). This is truly a teacher with a heart.

❖ 6 ❖

College was not a sure thing for Covello as it cost money. For most Italian families in East Harlem, college was not something to give thought to. With considerable encouragement from Mary Accurso and one of his English teachers at Morris High School, Covello made application for a Pulitzer Scholarship at Columbia University. It was his only way of going on. In August of 1907 he heard that he had won one of the scholarships. His mother, by then very ill, preparing in her own way for death, was very happy—though she had to this point been little involved in Covello's schooling. She died just before his classes began at Columbia, leaving six children, four of them quite young.

Winning a Pulitzer Scholarship to Columbia, which covered his expenses and provided him a fairly substantial monthly income, enabled Covello to do what he had long believed would be impossible. He did well academically, being initiated into Phi Beta Kappa in 1911, but he also found Columbia disappointing intellectually. It seemed to him to be little more than several additional years of high school. He noted in a 1964 interview, "The Columbia campus was an isolated community; social and contemporary problems were never discussed in classes" (Peebles, 1968, p. 94). Obviously, he wanted more than was available at most colleges and universities at this time.

Regardless of where Columbia was as an institution, Covello found himself going increasingly outward, to the dilemmas of his neighborhood. Long before college, he was engaged in tutoring activities at local settlement houses. He had also taught religious education courses for children and youth and coached youth soccer. Before the end of his freshman year, Covello picked up on some of his earlier work, teaching English to foreigners who were seeking citizenship. Unlike his earlier efforts, however, this was a more formal activity, in a well-established citizenship-training program. He was required to follow a prescribed format—speaking only in English, negating the language of the students. Following such a pattern, he found it very hard to get anyone to speak. "Finally," he noted, "I became impatient and let out a tirade of Italian, 'What is the matter with all of you? . . . Questa e una tavola. This is a table!' They stared at me and at each other. Then . . . a voice whispered, 'Pasquale, il professore e Italiano!'. . . After that it was easy" (p. 76). The experience influenced Covello a great deal. It seemed only logical to him that you would bring people— young or old—to English through their own language.

Covello also understood that these Italian immigrants wanted to learn English—so they could understand what was going on around them, possibly earn more money. He rejected the sentiment that had been so strong—"Those people won't learn English. If they don't want to learn English, they should return to Italy." Such a view didn't match the reality, but "Speak English" took hold. Today, the response to new immigrants is "English only," and legislation to make English "the official language" is moving through various legislative bodies. Many things remain the same. Those of us who work in and around schools need to be advocates for home languages. Our students need to see us standing with them in opposition to English-only proclamations.

Regarding his English language courses, Covello noted that some of the men began bringing their children with them "to ask my advice about a school situation or problem. . . . It was then that I realized how little these parents understood about school conditions and regulations affecting their children. . . . It became important for me to find out more about the problems they were unable to solve in becoming adjusted to a new way of life in a new country. And I could only do this through the use of native language" (p. 77). This was a lesson he took with him into his work in the schools.

Covello's response was all about respect, a willingness to join together with the students' struggles, to be in solidarity with them, to go beyond the surface appearances. Whereas many teachers move from distance, standing apart, to seeing their students as victims, needing to be understood (which isn't much of an improvement), Covello moved much further, actually joining the students, standing alongside them, being with them in their struggles. He refused to see the students as victims because they didn't see themselves as victims. I took a lot from Covello's stance of solidarity when I first read his autobiography. It affirmed for me my own efforts in those directions.

I thought about Covello recently when I met a young man in the subway I had worked with several years ago in a Boston high school. Phillipe told me that he was working for a security company in Harvard Square, saving money to pay for his car, hoping to enter a community college, considering marriage. The conversation then moved to the class I had taught and in which Phillipe had been one of thirty-nine students. He noted his surprise that I shook his hand each day and often asked him how things were going. I shared with him how much I appreciated the letter he had written me several months after the course ended in which he said, "You actually *wanted* to hear what I thought . . . you didn't have to listen to me but you *wanted* to." He understood that he was being respected and it mattered.

While at Columbia, Covello gained a larger view of the disparities of American life—the great wealth alongside extreme levels of poverty. He noted: "There was equality of opportunity, it was said, but in practice it did not seem to work out that way. I began to question why this had to be so. While I was never much interested in politics before,

I found myself now arguing social problems"(p. 89). Covello consciously began to listen to Socialist orators, finding his way to Norman Thomas's church and beginning to attend Socialist study groups. He remained troubled throughout his life by the exploitation of immigrants, African Americans, the poor, and the "individualism" that seemed to be invoked to support it.

Being fully engrossed in these college years with the cultural route of Italians in America, Covello got involved with the establishment, in 1910, of the East Harlem YMCA branch in a brownstone on East 116th Street. It quickly became an important community education center—with an outdoor basketball and handball court, a pool table, a kitchen, a small library, and meeting rooms. Evening classes in English and citizenship training for adults as well as tutoring programs for students in school were organized. There was also a music club and a literary club, and each Sunday afternoon, lectures and concerts were held. The focus of the library and the intellectual events was on Italian culture. It became a very inviting center for local immigrant families. While Covello dedicated several years to the growth and development of this East Harlem branch, he could not raise enough money to keep it open after the Central Y chose to withdraw in 1913 because "it was too small." The Y's interest, according to Covello, was in big, highly visible centers and large benefactors. The East Harlem Y, short-lived as it was, provided Covello another important outlet for his outwardness, his commitment to teaching in support of his community.

Covello's interest in his Italian roots continued as he went into teaching. By then, however, he was anxious to get young people more involved in their heritage. One of his involvements outside of school was the Young Men's Lincoln Club of Little Italy, which was designed to assist Italian-American youth in living more easily in two cultures—that of their parents and that associated with the school and American society. The idea, Covello noted, was "to acquaint these young [Italian] men with their Mediterranean culture and give them an appreciation of and pride in the country of their parents. . . ."

> We studied the accomplishments of such men as St. Francis, Savonarola, Galileo, Garibaldi, Da Vinci, Mazzini. We took up great events in American history: the discovery of Columbus, the landing at Plymouth Rock, the signing of the Declaration of Independence, William Penn and the Indians. We were striving to give these young men something more than they were getting from their teachers in the day school: an understanding of the relationship be-

tween these two cultures. And we tried to impress upon them that, instead of being ashamed or confused by the duality of their background, theirs was an especially rich heritage, of not only one culture but two—the old and new. (p. 104)

Later Covello would ask why the cultural studies that are so important remain outside of school. Over time, Covello got such work into the schools. But why should it have been so difficult? Why is it now so difficult to make cultural studies central to life in the schools rather than the kinds of things we do on occasion as activities for special days?

Like so many of us who work in the field of education, we were, as Covello was, teachers long before our baccalaureate degrees and teacher certification, able to stand alongside others, helping them see possibilities for their lives. As I read about Covello's early teaching experiences, I couldn't help reflect on my own.

In the neighborhood in which I grew up, almost all the younger children learned how to play outdoor games from me—baseball, football, basketball, soccer, hockey, four square, horseshoes, volleyball, newcomb, paddleball, tennis, badminton, dodgeball and kick-the-can, among others (and there *were* many others). There wasn't a game I didn't have a working knowledge of or was unable to actively teach with confidence. This kind of teaching continued throughout my high school and college years, extending beyond sports and recreational games to crafts, literature, reading and writing, community studies, and religious education.

What did I learn from all this early, pre-professional teaching? Most of all that teaching is not telling, that readiness for learning matters, that exemplars—actual, visible performances and products—are critical. Learning to play baseball meant in the end actually playing baseball; learning to read meant actually reading real books, real texts. Covello was in a similar place.   *Significance*

Covello understood that the curriculum of a school had to be connected to what students observed day in and day out in their communities. Moreover, it had to help students engage the dilemmas of their communities, prepare them to assume critical roles in change, to become active "citizens." He accepted Jean Piaget's challenge that schools should help students be in a position to change the world (Duckworth, 1996). This early teaching as a high school and college student was important to Covello's thinking about the need for a school to be a community institution. He also acknowledged that "the usual curriculum of our schools still does not seem to contribute in any significant manner to such training" (Covello, 1943, p. 136).

Covello clearly understood the power of identifying with a common struggle—the needs that actually existed in a community. He saw the school as a setting concerned with the continuous transformation and improvement of the community, an idea that John Dewey also developed fully. Such an aim seems large and noble compared with so much of what dominates the current discourse, filled with information-related mandates and threats of failure rooted in a host of tests.

❖ 7 ❖

The history of the United States is, in large measure, a history of immigration and migration. One would think that such a history would have brought about over the years a more sympathetic understanding of the dilemmas of being in a new country, a new setting, with many different customs and beliefs. That has not been the case. Those of us who are close to the earlier immigration/migration history understand how painful life was, especially for our mothers and fathers.

As we observe the new immigrants from the Caribbean, Southeast and East Asia, Mexico and Central America, we see so much of our own history, wishing it could be better, cringing as we hear new epithets and old, one would think worn-out, arguments about immigrants' "taking American jobs," as well as comments such as "Why don't *those* people learn to speak English?" A young high school student from Cambodia described to students of mine recently that the question "Why don't you people learn to speak English?" was especially stinging. "Why," she noted, "would we not want to, have to, learn to speak English?" Our schools should not let all of this pass unchallenged.

Looking back, it is clear that assimilation did not come easily for Southern Italians in the latter nineteenth and early twentieth centuries. This new land was not very hospitable. The "Little Italys" that formed in various urban centers were responses, forms of accommodation to the harsh conditions, a social-cultural refuge in which immigrants tried to recreate as much as possible of the old world.

Very few of the Italian immigrants in the 1880–1920 period came to engage in a profession, farming, or business. The great majority, almost regardless of the skills they might have developed at home, entered the labor market as unskilled workers to build the railroads and bridges, work the mills and the mines, staff the factories. Almost everything they did—except to engage in hard work—was new to them.

One of the curious elements of the schools in this heavy immigration period was, as I have noted, the reluctance to make use of the native languages or support the backgrounds of the immigrants—their historical and cultural contributions, their life patterns. The belief was that Americanization meant giving up the native tongue. While Covello, as an Italian, taught in settings where Italian students were increasing in numbers, and early on at DeWitt Clinton was asked to be the "caretaker" of Italian students by the principal, who was concerned about "all the difficulties these students were having in the school," his was not the usual situation. Many Italian parents, in fact, were convinced that special efforts were made to staff the schools their children attended with the lightest skinned, most blue-eyed, Protestant teachers available. Americanization was not very supportive of children's cultural roots.

In describing his own education in the schools, Covello recounted: "In all the four years I was at PS 83 as well as the 'Soup School,' I do not recall one mention of Italy or of the Italian language, or what famous Italians had done in the world. Pretty soon we got the idea that Italian meant something inferior" (Peebles, 1968, p. 84).

The established languages in the New York public schools, from 1896 to 1914, were German, French, and Latin. (Spanish was added in 1914.) There was virtually no discussion about whether Italian language might be helpful to Italian students in their ongoing learning or in their relationships with their parents. Covello entered the language debates early in his teaching, believing that "bilingualism" was an important goal. His constant talk about having the Italian language taught in the schools brought him considerable criticism. Many suggested to him, "You are keeping the boys foreigners." They also thought his focus on the Italian students was little more than "segregation," moving the Little Italys that were outside into the school. We still have these kinds of arguments in relation to the various ethnic studies programs that have become popular in some of our schools.

In contrast to such conventional thought, Covello saw the Italian language as the best vehicle for acculturation and as a means of bringing families together. In 1923, Italian was made an official language within the New York City curriculum, Covello became the head of an Italian department, and overnight, it seemed, Italian became DeWitt Clinton's most popular language. By 1926, over 500 students were enrolled in Italian language classes. Covello never gave up on his interests in bilingualism, arguing throughout his professional life for more teachers who spoke the immigrants' languages, who shared some of their experiences, who could engage them in all curricular areas, if necessary, in their language. While at Benjamin Franklin, he advocated specifically for more Spanish-speaking teachers because of the large influx of Puerto Ricans. I suspect, if he were still with us, he would be advocating for the various languages of the more recent immigrants from East Asia. He has left that challenge for those of us who wish to continue his important legacy. The challenge has grown over the past decade as bilingual programs have come under increasing attack—as "keeping people foreigners." We should know better by now.

Americanization was, in Covello's years, the goal of American society—the stance taken in relation to the immigrants. And schools were given the primary task of assuring that Americanization took hold. For immigrants, the schools' efforts were often understood as a means of separating children from their parents. It was easy for immigrant parents to believe that teachers were causing children to disrespect them and the knowledge they possessed. Most, primarily because of the language barrier, were kept away from the school, and provided little information.

In his popular *Changing Conceptions of Education*, Edward Cubberley (1909), one of the dominant educational figures of the day, wrote of Americanization: "[The goal] is to teach Anglo-Saxon concepts of righteousness, law and order and popular government" (p. 13). The textbooks were mirrors of such a view, filled with examples of how Americans did things, and Americans were clearly not Southern Italians. The text here was quite clear. All the virtues rested with the English speakers, "the Americans," not with the new immigrants from Southern and Eastern Europe. Further, "Speak English" campaigns were prominent in many of the schools "foreigners" attended. There are many school histories of this period that describe the awarding of "We Speak English" buttons and certificates "to children who signed pledges to speak English [at all times] and encourage others to do likewise" (Lintelman, 1986, p. 9).

This narrow view of Americanization, however, did not go fully unchallenged in the public and educational discourse. *The Melting Pot*, popularized in Israel Zangwill's 1908 play by that name, put forward the view that new people were being created in this American crucible through the alchemy of cultural integration. This "melting pot" formulation certainly had a more democratic ring to it, becoming a popular means of describing the fruits of immigration. In practice, however, it didn't change much that went on in the schools.

In contrast, Horace Kallen (1924) argued for a conception he called *cultural pluralism*, an acceptance of an American culture made up of many distinctive groups of people who retained much of their cultural base. He used the image of an orchestra to display his vision—many different instruments, with distinctive sounds, but together making an even more harmonious and vibrant sound. Covello was attracted to Kallen's vision, even as he doubted the country's capacity to adopt such a direction. By the end of the decade, Kallen's basic ideas flowed into what became an active Intercultural Education movement that was influential in many schools, promoting curricular reformation to include the stories of long-absent groups along with efforts to address racial, ethnic, and cultural conflicts.

Interested in these cultural issues, Covello became, in 1934, a board member of the Institute for Intercultural Education, which had been organized in Philadelphia by Rachel Davis DuBois, a pioneer in the human relations field. In 1936, Covello worked directly with the Institute on a study of racial attitudes at the Benjamin Franklin School, followed by a year of assembly programs that included Jewish rabbis, African American poets and writers, Japanese and Chinese actors, Puerto Rican storytellers and musicians. This was an effort aimed at providing education about various racial and ethnic groups. Additionally, teachers were provided intercultural training, mostly an exploration of personal attitudes as well as support for developing a more inclusive curriculum. The latter meant bringing new content into the curriculum as well as learning how to detect bias, being prepared to act on disrespectful language, understanding more fully the meaning of fairness. We have few schools today that make this kind of integrated effort to address matters of diversity.

While at Columbia and in all the years that followed, Covello read everything he could about Italian culture, about conditions in Southern Italy, about matters of immigration.[1] No longer ready to hide, he ex-

1. Covello presented in 1943 an impressive doctoral thesis (at New York University) entitled The Social Background of the Italo-American School Child: A Study of the Southern Italian Mores and Their Effect on the School Situation in Italy and America. Later published by the E. J. Brill Press, it remains one of the best accounts of conditions in Southern Italy, the source of most of the Italian immigration to the United States.

pressed what it meant to be an Italian, an immigrant in America. He no longer accepted the anti-immigrant discourse that was growing stronger in 1912 and 1913 and led to debates about closing off the flow from Southern and Eastern Europe. He never lost that powerful voice on behalf of the strangers in this land.

Why did Covello, or why should any other immigrant or person from a long-disenfranchised population, have to wait so long for the confidence to speak about his or her cultural base? Why must any person be made to feel inferior, or lesser? Even as I know that new immigrants are bombarded by the rhetoric of U.S. nationalism and "the American way of life," their cultural background should continue to matter and not be pushed aside.

In 1913, one of Covello's Italian-American students came to him with a fully developed plan for a cultural entity associated with the school to foster cultural knowledge and pride—"Il Circolo Italiano." The student noted:

> There are many of us now at DeWitt Clinton, . . . some like me who were born in Italy and those who were born in America. We are many but there is nothing to hold us together. We need a club— special for those who are of our blood. . . . "Why?" I asked. . . . "Why do you feel that such a club would do any good?"
>
> He took some scribbled notes out of his pocket and smoothed them out on the table. "The Circolo. Il Circolo Italiano we call it. We need a club like this to make the Italian-American student understand that he doesn't have to be ashamed that his mother and father are Italian. He will find out that friends all over New York, who live just like him, think just like him, come to school for the same reasons. He will learn that instead of belonging just to the block or the neighborhood, he belongs to something bigger, much, much bigger." (pp. 109–110)

Covello agreed to be the faculty advisor of what became by 1920 a citywide movement. The primary purpose of Il Circolo was "self education, social or civic service [and] bridging the gap between the old generation and the new and between the Italian and American Culture" (Peebles, 1968, p. 136). Beyond the school day, within the Circolo, Italian-American students read Italian literature, studied reports about the conditions their families left behind in Italy, and gained greater knowledge of the Italian language. The Circolo was also a setting for social fellowship, which many Italian-American students, as a minority population in DeWitt Clinton, did not experience within the school. As Covello noted, they had little contact with the non-Italian students. In these social and cultural functions, it was an early ethnic studies program. It wasn't long before *Il Circolo* was asking that Italian be made an official language in the curriculum, that Italian writers assume greater prominence in the literature curriculum, that Italian scientists be acknowledged in science courses, and more Italian teachers be appointed. Students were not suggesting that *all* teachers needed to be Italian, that they couldn't learn from non-Italian teachers or that their learning would necessarily be greater if they were taught *only* by Italian teachers. They were, however, asking for greater balance.

This issue remains with us and represents, in fact, a serious problem. The percentage of teachers of color in our current schools is hardly representative of the students in the schools. In 1997, approximately 14% of all teachers are of color, a percentage that hasn't grown much since 1972. There is little to indicate that we are likely to see much change over the next decade, even as the population of students from African American, Afro-Caribbean, Hispanic, Asian, and Native American backgrounds is expanding greatly, likely to be the majority of all students in the public schools early in the next century.

Dropout rates for students of color, especially for African Americans, Native Americans, and Hispanics, range in many settings from 35% to 55%. This is obviously a personal disaster for large numbers of young people; it is also a social and economic disaster for their communities and the country. In interviews with many of these young men and women, they speak of uncaring schools, of seeing little connection between the content of schools and their lives, of settings that are disrespectful of their families, of not having teachers to whom they can relate. Seeing more faculty who share their backgrounds, who see in them themselves, who hold out lifelines of possibility, has to make a difference. Greater balance among the teaching staff could make a difference.

In schools with better balance among the teacher population, there is more talk of students' strengths, less talk about "pathological conditions" among families and neighborhoods. All the talk of victimization is itself victimizing. When there is greater balance, the forest of the schools becomes more visible. Curriculum materials assume a broader range, more inclusivity. The discourse tends to be more respectful.

Seeing more brown-eyed Italian-speaking teachers in the New York City schools of the 1920s—persons who knew their students' experiences, who could relate easily to them and their families, who could serve as role models within the pluralism of the society—might have kept more Italians in the schools. As it was, only one of twenty graduated from high school. As I recount this story, I look out at our schools filled with the new immigrants from Mexico and Central America and Haiti and Southeast Asia. What has changed for them? Are they receiving the support they need to survive at high levels in this society?

Thirty percent of the students in the elementary school and the high school I attended were African American and Mexican-American, but I never saw anything but white (mostly Northern European in background) teachers. I received a good academic education, but as I think about democracy writ large, it wasn't as good as it needed to have been. My African American and Mexican-American classmates didn't fare as well; few completed high school and those who did weren't in any of the courses I was in.

Helping students stay in school to graduation was one of the major service activities of the *Circolo*—especially in the 1920s. It involved tutoring and home visits to encourage parents to support their children's attendance and active participation in school. Students in *Il Circolo* also taught English to immigrants in the various settlement houses and coordinated recreational programs for children in the various playgrounds.

One of the measures of success of the *Circolo* was the continued involvement of graduates, many of whom maintained their service work in the settlement houses and participated in various cultural activities at the school and in the Italian communities. A popular product of the DeWitt Clinton *Circolo* was *Il Foro* (The Forum), a journal devoted to Italian culture and written in both Italian and English. Its special 1921 issue on Dante, commemorating the 600th anniversary of Dante's death, was widely circulated and honored, even by the Italian government. By the mid 1920s, *Il Circolo Italiano* at DeWitt Clinton involved over 300 boys. It was virtually a school within the school.

Alongside the *Circolo*, Covello helped organize at DeWitt Clinton the Italian Parent-Teachers Association. It was a means of getting Italian parents together to help them understand the school and its purposes. Parents also were encouraged to keep their children in school and to consider college.

Covello understood, however, that this Parent-Teachers Association needed a social side, getting parents out of their homes, in contact with others. Given his own experience, especially with his mother, Covello knew that immigrant life could be lonely and isolating.

"Italian Nights" were held at least twice a year at the school or in a neighborhood setting. Typically these Italian nights featured an Italian play performed by *Circolo* members, followed by a dance and refreshments. Teachers at DeWitt Clinton slowly learned what Covello understood—"that the unit of education was not merely the child. The unit of education must be the family" (p. 158).

The *Circolo*, begun at DeWitt Clinton to support students of Italian parentage, was developed later in Benjamin Franklin for Puerto Rican students with similar goals and activities. In addition, Covello organized the Hispano-American Education Bureau, similar in purpose to the earlier Italian-American Education Bureau, as an agency aimed at promoting

> a better understanding among residents of the United States of the life, culture and institutions of our fellow Americans to the south, as well as to assist Spanish-American residents of the United States to solve such problems as may militate against their securing the mental ease and physical comforts to which they are entitled while residing in our midst, and specifically in East Harlem, one of the most underprivileged areas of the City of New York. This can be best attained by cooperating with them in securing such educational, vocational, and health guidance as only trained educators thoroughly conversant with and sympathetic toward the Spanish-American outlook can give. (Covello, quoted in Peebles, 1968, p. 239)

Covello's commitment to parents and his respect for language also come through as he describes the following encounter:

> I am there, once again at my office at Franklin. I see the careworn face of a little Puerto Rican woman, aged in the fields of her native island. She has come to see me on some matter relating to her son.
>
> "Señora," I say to her in Spanish, "sit down. Make yourself comfortable and we will talk about Miguel and his future." And to the boy, also in Spanish, "You sit down over there and do not interrupt us while I talk to your mother." The only language of education is the language which people can understand—no matter where it originates. To this simple Puerto Rican woman I have suddenly become more than the principal of an English-speaking high school. I am a human being who understands and is trying to help her. In the eyes of the boy I have given respect and status to

his parent. The process of education has been translated into human terms. (p. 267)

In contrast to this account, so many others who are poor and speak
another language find little respect. They find themselves unwelcome
partners in their children's education.

❖ 8 ❖

Maxine Greene (1978) has reminded us of our need for "wide-
awakeness," an ongoing consciousness of the complexities of the
world we inhabit. She admonishes us as teachers to be more coura-
geous; to speak about injustice; to raise questions about practices that
are not inclusive, that don't enlarge what is possible for all children; to
work toward schools and communities that respect diversity, that
support children, young people, and their families, providing them
means "to transform the world." This may seem to be a large obliga-
tion. Yet our students need to know that we care deeply about the
world around us, that we stand for something important. Our actions
matter. This represents the moral part of our work.

Covello addressed the essence of Greene's wide-awakeness early
in his teaching at DeWitt Clinton High School. Though DeWitt Clinton
was acknowledged in 1912 as "a highly successful school," providing
its students a strong academic program, Covello worried, almost immediately after accepting a teaching position, about "the steady flow
of failures and drop-outs" (p. 96). He was especially aware of how few
children of Italian immigrants were succeeding academically or managing to persist through graduation. While the general view at DeWitt
Clinton, and probably at most other high schools at the time, was that
"secondary schools aren't for everyone," Covello had a different understanding of the purpose of a public high school. He was unwilling,
for example, to blame the students for the failures they suffered or
support the view that high school graduation was important only for
those with college aspirations or those whose parents spoke English.

Covello asked early in his career, "Who is responsible for these
failures? For that matter, why should there be failures at all?" (p. 79).
Rather than starting first with the students as the source of failure,
Covello directed his attention to the school. Was it doing enough to
support *all* students? Did the curriculum match student interests?
make connections to the cultural backgrounds of students? relate to
issues that mattered in the community? In many ways those were

revolutionary questions. What if we asked such questions systemati-
cally today in our schools? Moreover, he noted with regard to the
schools that "everything is cut and dried. The only trouble is that the
student is far from being cut and dried. He is an individual, with individual needs and abilities" (p. 99). I think teachers know this. Yet,
given the school cultures surrounding them, they have a difficult time
making this the dominant understanding of schools, working from
that perspective.

I recall vividly, in my second year of secondary school teaching, in
1957, hearing the senior English teacher say, with pride it seemed, that
50% of her students received failing grades for that particular grading
period. Even though she was not talking to me, I still managed to blurt
out: "How could that be possible?" Needless to say, we shared few
words thereafter. Should teachers and schools bear most of the responsibility for student failure? The question is clearly vexing. While I
know that there are *some* students who close themselves off to the possibilities of learning successfully in schools, I have remained convinced
from my earliest years as a teacher that teachers and schools *should* assume the principal responsibility for what happens to the students—
especially in regard to failure. If all their efforts were directed toward
student success, making sure they knew their students well enough to
engage them intensively, understanding that they might have to scaf-
fold learning activities in different ways for different students and being ready to organize their schools and pedagogies to *fit the students*
(rather than continuing to ask students *to fit the schools*), there would be
far fewer failures. Deborah Meier (1986) has suggested, in this regard,
that one of the reasons for Central Park East's success has been its ongoing willingness to change everything if that would make it more
possible for a particular student to succeed. That seems to me to be a
reasonable stance.

Covello noted later in his career, "To me, failure at any age, but
particularly during adolescence is something the seriousness of which
can not be exaggerated. . . . The solution must be found within the
schools" (p. 174). Unfortunately, the tendency in schools as we move
into the twenty-first century is to invoke more toughness about standards that are externally defined, that often don't relate to the students
themselves, believing again that high school may not be for everyone.
A willingness to accept failure may become again more common as
well as even more disastrous.

La Escuela Nueva, a school in Juan Domingo, just outside San Juan
in Puerto Rico, has a tradition of asking each year about everything it

does, "What does it mean for the students?" Some of the following questions are raised: Why do we begin the school day at 8:00 A.M.? Why not 9:00 A.M.? Why do we begin with a schoolwide community activity? Why not start with everyone in individual classrooms? Why do we do an annual community survey? What do we learn that we didn't already know? Why do we make Juan Domingo so central to all our studies? Why do we have every student in community service? Why do we organize around a common theme? Why do we persist with a full range of arts programs? And I have raised only a small number of the questions posed. The process is, of course, a means of reaffirming the school's purposes on behalf of the students, but it is also a serious invitation to change practices if it would make something better—socially and academically—for the students. Such a stance, broadly emulated, might help us get to a more constructive place in regard to our work.

Teachers in schools wishing to consider other possibilities for themselves and their students might begin by asking "What if?" questions. What if we organized around two integrated courses each day rather than seven discipline-bound courses? What if we had a writing workshop each day rooted exclusively in students' experience, unencumbered by any sentence starters, prompts, worksheets, or workbooks, that gave attention to voice? What if all students painted from kindergarten through high school? What if all conversations about students began with a description of their strengths? Such "What if?" questions, and this list can certainly be added to, could help break the current conventions of schools.

Early in his teaching career, Covello noted to close friends:

> I instruct about one hundred and forty boys every day, but what exactly do I know about them? I watch them. They're like shadows as far as we, the teachers, are concerned—coming out of nowhere every morning and at three o'clock going back into nowhere. How can we really do our jobs as teachers unless we know something about the pupils we are trying to teach? (pp. 97–98)

The Coalition of Essential Schools, a contemporary effort to join teachers in reforming secondary schools, has made of Covello's very wide-awake observation and question a mantra: "It is impossible to teach students well if you don't know them well." Covello, though, went beyond the contemporary view of "knowing the students well." It meant for him more than knowing their intellectual inclinations, the questions that mattered to them, the books they were inclined to read, their dispositions to inquiry, their modes of engaging fresh content, all of which he would acknowledge to matter greatly. To know the students well also meant knowing something of their cultural roots, where they and their parents came from, what their living conditions were like, what kinds of generational issues were being confronted by students and their parents, whether the students were receiving medical attention, eating enough, were safe enough. That kind of knowing meant hours of personal interaction with students and significant connections with the parents of the students. Can we make such knowing central to our work as teachers?

At a later point in his career, Covello explained more fully what he had learned about "knowing the students." He writes:

> I learned how much there was to know about the people I was trying to teach. I stopped talking at my students, lecturing to classes. I developed the habit of listening, trying to penetrate the inner world of the people facing me. When talking to one of my boys, the first question I asked was where he lived. I sought to project myself outside and beyond the walls of the school and visualize the block where he lived, the home from which he came and the conversation that took place in the evening around his dinner table. Only by understanding him could I teach him. (p. 178).

I understand that Covello's need to know the students may appear extreme in the current climate of schools. There is, for example, a good deal of talk today about the schools' having taken on too much—that a social services agenda (certainly Covello's stance) has overtaken the academic agenda. The new discourse focuses on "academic standards," which have come increasingly to be long lists of things students are expected to know or be able to do. Such a direction grows from the belief that our students are not being prepared sufficiently for the "new global economy." By and large, this standards movement is more about standardization than standards, and it tends in most cases to look right past the students teachers meet day in and day out in their classrooms. Covello understood, as have successful teachers over the years, that students who come to school hungry, sick, starving for an adult to talk with, and in need of greater personal guidance find it very difficult to attend to the learning agenda. A breakfast program in many of our schools is absolutely essential. It was the case in 1920 and it is the case today. Ties to social service agencies that can supplement the attention schools can provide are often crucial. Covello's vision of a "community school" envisioned close ties; our schools today need those connections. Covello also understood that it makes no sense to pit social and academic matters against one another. Social *and* academic issues are *always* present. There may be times when greater attention will have to be given to social concerns, while *not* ignoring academic matters completely; and there will be times when the academic focus will dominate, while *not* ignoring social concerns fully.

In his early DeWitt Clinton days, Covello raised money for what he called a "Social Welfare Committee." It was an activity that continued at Benjamin Franklin, providing support for students who needed health services beyond those provided in the school—shoes, coats, glasses, car fare, and family food supplements. In the depression years of the 1930s, some 300 boys per month were provided services from this fund. The impetus for this activity, as was the case for much that Covello did, grew out of conversations with students. He claimed to have learned a great deal from his students' questions and concerns. His interactions with them were, in this regard, authentic. The Social Welfare Committee had its beginnings with a student's account of his father's death and his worries about being able to continue with school. The various tutoring and big-brother programs that were also prominent in the Benjamin Franklin school grew from what Covello describes as students' sense of being failures because learning English wasn't coming along easily or reading was a problem.

Working out of such experience, Covello also asked teachers at Benjamin Franklin to view themselves as counselors for the students, friends in need, persons ready to make home visits, to engage the students in their fullness. It was in such close relationships that Covello believed teachers would know of their students' difficulties and could then do something constructive on their behalf. They could provide help with reading or math. They could take an active role in assuring that all students were successful, able to do what they most wanted to do. The "whole child" mattered. In schools associated with the current Coalition of Essential Schools, it is common for "advisories" to be established, small settings in which all teachers become counselors, friends to students, persons who establish close relationships with a small group of students and their families. These advisories match well what Covello had in mind. Efforts in such directions should be more commonplace.

Covello thought it was important to live in the community, close to his students. This, he noted, made it possible for him to see his students and their families in the streets and to visit their homes. He conveys in his autobiography and various speeches how often he had important conversations with students and their parents outside of school, in their more natural environment. He clearly valued these exchanges. And he was, as students recalled, a frequent visitor in their homes. It meant as well that community issues affecting his students were also his issues, affecting him personally as well as professionally.

Covello thought it was natural, for example, to make housing a major issue for the Benjamin Franklin Community High School to assume leadership around, because it mattered to his students and their families—as well as to him. In addition, he personally got involved, as a teacher, in organizing neighborhood libraries in the East Harlem community—because he lived there and could speak easily to his students, parents, and community members about the importance of such libraries and their collective need to help staff them. Moreover, that East Harlem should have better medical facilities was clear to Covello, another issue for the school to consider critical because he lived in East Harlem and knew a good deal about community needs. Making medical care a schoolwide issue also seemed natural to Covello as he came to believe that the school's curriculum should be connected to community concerns. He understood well the meaning of a pedagogy of place.

Covello noted very early in his career that a productive teaching-learning exchange had to be constructed on more than a series of academic courses with little relationship to the world beyond schools.

> The subject both fascinated and tormented me. Without being quite sure of what it was, I began to sense a purpose in life which transcended the simple business of teaching the rudiments of a foreign language [Covello's teaching field]. Little by little other problems in education began to press upon me. (p. 98)

Covello noted that so much of what went on in school was about "control"—keeping the students busy, trying to "channel their boundless energy" as they moved from teacher to teacher, class to class every forty-five minutes, "while outside the sun is shining, the air is brisk, and the river glistens" (p. 99).

In thinking about his work as a teacher, Covello often went back to his own autobiography as a student in elementary and secondary school. "Little by little," he says, "I began to relive my own youth in terms of the students before me. I tried to see the process of education from their viewpoints" (p. 99). He came to the realization that most of what the school offered was about a future life—"it will be good for you someday." He understood, however, that "the boys were vitally alive now, concerned only with the present" (p. 99). John Dewey expressed a similar view, noting that the best education for a future life is to concentrate on making what is being done now the best that is possible, that what is being studied must make a difference to students as they are living their lives in the present. Such a perspective seems so clearly right. Yet we persist, it seems, with admonitions about how students "will *need* this" at a later time, when they are in college, when they are mothers or fathers.

The lessons that Covello learned early in his career were lessons that I also learned early in my teaching. As much as I expected the content of American History, World History, and Government (the courses I taught at the secondary level) to be at the center of my work, the students—their needs, interests, confusions, dilemmas—always took precedence. As was certainly the case for Covello, I can think of hundreds of students who made an impression on me that went far beyond the courses I taught. I'll share one experience from my fourth year of teaching at a very large, integrated secondary school in Lansing, Michigan, that still influences my thoughts about the importance of knowing the students well, making connections to interests that go beyond the normal curriculum.

I had two brothers in my tenth-grade history course who were very quiet, doing too little with the course, often late to class. When I talked with them about being late, they told me they ran traps in the morning and sometimes it took longer than they anticipated. Since we were in the city, nothing about the traps made sense to me. As it turned out, they lived outside the city in a swamp area. They asked without hesitation if I would like to walk their trap line with them. How could I say no? We made arrangements for me and my two-and-a-half-year-old son to go to their house on a subsequent Saturday morning. Getting to the house meant driving through parts of the swamp on a perilous road that gave me many second thoughts. It was all worth it. There was life here I didn't know existed. The traps were empty that Saturday morning, but I learned about beavers and muskrats, their habitats and their economic value. I also saw two young men who were different than they were in school—talkative, confident, happy. It was the beginning of a most engaging three-year conversation.

These two young men were first-class naturalists, who comprehended, it seemed, everything possible to know about the growth of plants and the habits of various wildlife. Yet, as I learned, they were struggling with their biology class (and their teacher never did learn about their wilderness lives). They were also excellent landscapers and builders. And there was little they couldn't do with an automobile— whether engine or body work. Moreover, they produced wooden bowls and wood sculptures that were truly works of art. (Their woodworking teacher, whom I met at one of their exhibits, *did* know a great deal about their talents. He also was a model for the kind of teacher I hoped to become, the ultimate exemplar of the teacher-as-coach.) My point in this, and I have told only a very short part of the story, is that I found these young men's abilities and understandings inspiring, yet they were barely making it at the school, did not see themselves as exceptional learners, and were given virtually *no* encouragement to believe they could be successful academically or consider any postsecondary education.

What if their strengths had been a basis for their education? As it was, these young men, and I suspect large numbers of others, were invisible to many teachers in the school. The need to know my students well, to be in a position to work from their strengths, their interests, their intentions, has stayed with me. It still animates my work as a teacher. It also shapes some of the ways I think about school structures, leading me increasingly to believe that we need to consider smaller school communities with smaller numbers of students working with a core of teachers who plan together, who gain individual and collective insights into the students they work with in common, who can engage the discourse of curriculum and standards, for example, with the seriousness such matters deserve, with the students they know well the focus of their attention.

❖ 9 ❖

Standardized tests have become so commonplace in the schools that we often believe they have been with us forever, possibly coming to us from classical Greece. They are, however, relatively recent aspects of schooling, dating back only to the beginning of the twentieth century. Their history is related in large measure to a desire to differentiate among people in regard to intelligence and academic achievement. World War I recruits and draftees provided an extremely large sample (some 1,700,000) on whom to try out the new testing instruments, which became after the war a central feature of the schooling experience. Rather than seeing the differences between recent immigrants and those who were native born as differences in language and cultural familiarity, the testers saw differences in intelligence and aptitude. That 79% of Italians scored poorly—at the "feeble minded" level—was an indication that Italian immigration might have been a mistake, endangering the country.

After World War I, these tests came to affect Americans of all ages, in all fields; however, they came down most heavily on the young, those between the ages of three and twenty-one. But the larger burden fell on those who were poor and/or racially, ethnically, or culturally different, primarily because they have tended to score, on average, below others. Harvard psychologist David McClelland (1973) suggests that standardized tests have been so thoroughly ingrained into American schools that "it is a sign of backwardness not to have test scores in the school records of children." It would be good if we saw the continued use of these tests and the power we vest in them as the real sign of backwardness.

Covello viewed the tests, commonly used by 1920 in New York's schools, as a "plague." He noted:

> I will never forget one of those testing periods. Several hundred boys were tested at the lunchroom tables. The tests all had a time limit. The examiner stood on the platform with a stopwatch and a whistle, ready to signal the beginning and end of each test. . . . Even to those of us without specialized training in psychology, it was obvious these tests could not accomplish all that was claimed for them. (p. 150)

As I read Covello's account, I was drawn back to my first experience as a teacher having to give a standardized test. The "examiner" was at the schools' intercom mike, Oz-like, giving instructions to teachers and students in eighty classrooms. It was "1984" in 1957. We were all automatons. The students knew, I am sure, that I was extremely uncomfortable, visibly upset. It was about as unnatural as anything in a school could be. Who would take any of the results seriously? Yet the results went into the students' records, markers of their "innate abilities."

Noting that boys of Italian parentage scored lower than others, Covello exclaimed to his wife: "How is this? Do you mean to tell me that this [graph of results] is supposed to be conclusive evidence that my boys have less brains? I don't believe it. My experience does not bear this out. I am not convinced" (p. 150).

Covello *shouldn't* have been convinced. The tests were flawed. Their claims should not have been accepted. Writing in *The Crisis*, W. E. B. DuBois (1920) suggested that the tests were just one more effort to prove "scientifically" that Northern Europeans were superior to all others. He notes, with regard to the Army tests related to "Negroes":

> For these tests were chosen 4,730 Negroes from Louisiana and Mississippi and 28,052 white recruits from Illinois. The result? Do you need to ask? . . . The intelligence of the average Southern Negro is equal to that of a 9-year-old white boy and that we should arrange our educational program to make waiters, porters, scavengers and the like of most Negroes. (p. 1183)

Walter Lippmann, writing in the *New Republic* (1922), wrote that

> Intelligence is not an abstraction like length and weight; it is an exceedingly complicated notion which nobody has yet succeeded in defining. . . . If the impression takes root that these tests really measure intelligence, that they contribute a sort of last judgment on the child's capacity, that they reveal "scientifically" his predetermined ability, then it would be a thousand times better if all the intelligence testers and their questionnaires were sunk without warning in the Sargasso Sea.

By 1924, in spite of all the doubts, the tests took hold. The testers presented their data to congressional committees, which were apparently convinced that the test scores meant something to worry about. Immigration was effectively stopped—with extremely low quotas for Southern and Eastern Europeans (who tended to score low on the various tests of the day and were labeled less desirable). It is bad enough that the tests affected immigration policy, but they have also affected negatively over many years the educational possibilities of large numbers of children, especially those who came from poor families, whose primary language was not English, or who were nonwhite. The recently published, surprisingly popular *Bell Curve*, by Richard Herrnstein and Charles Murray (1996), suggests that the matter of test scores and family background remains potent, which brings us back to the old arguments about genetic differences among racial and ethnic groups. Moreover, tests are again being used for purposes of promotion and graduation. This should worry all educators, as there is little evidence that such directions enhance student learning and considerable evidence that poor children and children of color are negatively affected. The work of Fairtest, an organization devoted to reform in relation to testing practices, has been particularly important in raising critical issues related to educational testing. But reform won't come until teachers, school administrators, and parents join in the struggle to reduce the power of externally devised tests.

❖ 1 0 ❖

In our classrooms today, teachers are looking out increasingly at students of many racial, linguistic, and cultural backgrounds. In many respects, our schools have never been as universal nor our population so varied. While Covello did not face as much diversity as currently exists, the issues were, nonetheless, not so different. Race, language, and cultural matters, alongside severe problems of housing, health care, and discrimination certainly dominated life in and around Covello's schools.

The discourse of multiculturalism is large at the present time, but it is played out mostly in the form of supplementary literature or regularly scheduled days, weeks, or months devoted to particular racial, ethnic, or cultural groups. This is clearly an advance, but it remains only a marginal response. What I have found most prevalent in the schools around race and cultural matters, however, is silence. Can we really believe that the barriers that now exist, that keep us from achieving the democratic ideals, the social justice, the economic progress that we hold out in our public discourse, will ever fall away without confronting more directly matters of race in the schools and in the society? How many more generations of silence can we endure? As it is, inquiries into matters of race in schools, colleges, and universities are awkward, guilt-ridden, sometimes hostile, but mostly absent. Where beyond schools and college classrooms are young people to learn to discuss matters of race with intelligence and sensitivity? How else but through active consideration of race will teachers and administrators in schools assume a higher level of awareness and take more seriously the effects of inequitable educational opportunity? I continue in this regard to be surprised by the denial of differential education for students of color—overplacement in special education and in lower-level courses, higher levels of suspension, lower graduation rates, higher dropout rates. When will such problems matter enough to actually do something about them? They don't exist by chance.

Covello was unusually sensitive to racial and cultural differences. He had heard enough of "wop" and "dago" to know that "kike," "nigger," and "spick" were closely related, that any effort to diminish another person was in itself diminishing. Race and culture were subjects to talk about, not hide.

One of the committees formed at the Benjamin Franklin Community High School was the Racial Committee. It had as a central purpose changing attitudes by constructing within the school more intercultural curriculum; assuring integrated clubs, committees, and social events; and encouraging in the community larger forums for discussion about issues relating to ethnicity and race.

By 1938, the school's curriculum, in every subject field, had intercultural content. It was a matter of genuine conversation in department meetings and in classrooms. Teachers assumed responsibility for learning more about their students and their cultural backgrounds. This is the kind of effort we should have more of today in every classroom and school.

Major conferences on racial and ethnic group relations were organized at the school. Two that received considerable public notice were the "Greater New York Conference on Racial and Cultural Relations in the United States" (in 1942) and "The Conference on Racial Conflict" (in 1943). Conference sponsors, beyond the Benjamin Franklin Racial Committee, were the National Association for the Advancement of Colored People, the American Jewish Council, the National Conference of Christians and Jews, the National Urban League and the American Committee for the Protection of the Foreign Born (Peebles, 1968).

Daniel Patrick Moynihan, currently New York's senior senator, provided as a high school student a set of resolutions to the 1942 Conference on Racial and Cultural Relations on behalf of the Benjamin Franklin Racial Committee. They were as follows: an end to racial segregation in the armed forces; the merging of Negro and white blood banks by the Red Cross; an increase in teachers representing various racial and cultural groups; and the appointment of a Director of Intercultural Education to support teachers in New York schools to promote intergroup understanding (Peebles, 1968). From a distance, it is hard not to be impressed by the fact that such issues were common enough to be discussed in the school setting and formulated as resolutions for debate. How many schools today are ready to examine racial attitudes in their schools and communities? or consider ways of assuring that teachers are more representative of local populations? or call for an end to discriminatory employment practices against certain racial or ethnic groups? or seek evidence about whether there is differential treatment of people in the criminal justice system or the health care systems? Most of us could add to this set of questions.

Covello noted of these large conferences, and other similar forums held in the East Harlem community:

> In recent years, there has been a tendency to isolate youth in "youth movements" and "youth groups." For some purposes, this is an excellent idea; but, in working out major problems in community life, both young people and old people should have a share. Both will learn much from the school, which assumes the leadership; and each will learn from the other. (quoted in Peebles, 1968, p. 274)

East Harlem underwent many changes over Covello's time in that community. Its large Italian population was being replaced in the late 1930s by new Puerto Rican immigrants and African Americans from the South who had come to New York as part of the Great Migration. Transition times in communities have often produced in our cities racial-ethnic tensions. Covello clashed often with the media and their accounts of East Harlem as "dangerous," "gang-ridden," and "violent." Covello wrote in the aftermath of press reports of interethnic conflict in East Harlem in the late 1930s:

> As guardian of community prestige, the school had to take a stand. I wrote a long letter to the paper that had editorialized on East Harlem, trying to present an accurate picture of conditions there, making a plea for understanding of our problems and the work we were trying to do to improve conditions.
>
> "As you may know, we have about thirty-four different racial and nationality strains in this single community. There are many problems connected with the life of the community that require sympathetic and intelligent handling. . . . I am firmly convinced that the solution does not lie in blanket condemnations of foreign-born communities or in the application of police force to periodic outbreaks of violence caused by conditions that are not understood by the general public." (p. 222)

When ethnic and racial tensions were particularly high in East Harlem, Covello, joined by student leaders, often went out into the community to talk with youth. He noted regarding one of these occasions:

> We would just stop and talk to people, regardless of color or nationality, telling them that we were from Benjamin Franklin High School and interested to know why people in the same neighborhood couldn't live peacefully together. . . .
>
> Occasionally we did encounter resentment. Usually it was from the Italians, and I would take over. One group of younger Italian workmen argued against the Puerto Ricans coming into the neighborhood and working for less wages. "They're not like us. We're American. We eat meat at least three times a week. What do they eat? Beans! So they work for beans. That's why we have trouble here."
>
> I asked them, "What do you think your parents ate when they came to America? You don't want to remember. I was there. *Pasta e fasul*," I said. "Beans and macaroni—and don't forget it. Don't forget that other people used to say the same things about your mothers and fathers that you now say about the Puerto Ricans." (p. 223)

Good-will demonstrations were also common fare, activities that joined students and community people. Covello discussed one such event in 1938:

> Better than two thousand persons attended. Both Italian and Puerto Rican leaders spoke in English and Italian and Spanish, urging cooperation and understanding and friendship for the sake of the community as a whole. The school was represented by [large numbers of students] . . . all of whom gave the viewpoint of the student on racial equality. (pp. 223–224)

The migration of Puerto Ricans into New York City, especially into East Harlem, was especially large after the Second World War. Covello moved quickly to organize a variety of educational programs, hoping to bring more receptivity to the Puerto Ricans than Italians and other Southern and Eastern European immigrants had received. He particularly wanted to make sure the newly arriving Puerto Ricans knew about all the social and educational services that were available to them.

I was reminded when reading Covello's story of an effort in Revere, Massachusetts, to make the entry of a new population smoother, more hospitable. When the principal of an all-white, fully English-speaking school learned that close to two hundred Cambodian children would be in the school in the fall, he started a process aimed at inclusion and social learning that went far beyond the norm. The principal and teachers decided that it was critical for everyone in the school—children, teachers, custodians, secretaries, lunchroom workers—to know who these Cambodian children were, where they had come from, and why they were coming to Revere. "Getting ready for the Cambodian children" became the full curriculum for several months, the basis for virtually all studies. The train of normal coverage was stopped. Those in the school community learned how to speak to the Cambodian children, and also gained considerable knowledge about their cultural patterns as well as their suffering. As part of their preparation, they learned about prejudice and the harm that prejudice brings to those who are different. They also learned how prejudice disrupts communities—whether schools or neighborhoods or cities. Their learning had meaning because it grew out of important social values and commitments related to equity, justice, respect for others, and human dignity, along with a willingness to make decisions surrounding such values and commitments. It made a visible difference. In the world of contemporary schools, it was an unusual response. It ought to be the *usual*. Such entries into the world should constitute a large share of the curriculum. It is the kind of work that builds for students social capacity—that sense of being able to make a difference in their communities, that causes them to see what they do as being vital, that they are genuine resources. It also relates to the ongoing concern for democracy. Covello understood this well. It is a lesson we all need to understand.

❖ 1 1 ❖

What does it mean for teachers to work together? Can some unified work be pursued? Covello made it clear that "we had to prepare our students for the very serious business of living and sharing in the responsibilities of society" (p. 205). As he saw it, everyone in the school had to pull together around such a purpose.

I cite the following account from the early work at the Benjamin Franklin Community High School as an example of joint work.

In the English Department, Austin Works channeled literature in the direction of books that gave the pupil a realistic picture of the world he lived in, as well as what was expected of him in return. Along with Shakespeare and Milton and Scott, the student was given writers such as Upton Sinclair, Lincoln Steffens and Ida Tarbell, who dealt with contemporary social problems.

Social-study classes stressed the theme "Know Your Community!"

The Art Department worked out a huge map of East Harlem, carefully outlining individual blocks. From this original which hung in my office, duplicates of a smaller size were printed and distributed to the various departments of the school and civic organizations of the neighborhood, to be used for their own purposes.

Slowly, on the master map, we began to accumulate information which, in turn, was fed out to the smaller maps. Before anything else, we wanted to know where our students lived. In varying colors to indicate nationality, we spotted them on the map and were astonished to find distributions and concentrations of population never before realized. As part of their social-studies experience, the boys took to the streets after hours with pencil and paper to gather statistical information about their neighborhood which the Art Department, in terms of symbols, transferred to the master map.

The map showed that in East Harlem there were forty-one churches and missions, twenty-two political clubs, nine labor organizations, five hundred and six candy stores, two hundred sixty-two barber shops. There were twenty-eight liquor stores, one hundred fifty-six bars, twenty-six junk shops, six hundred eighty-five grocers, three hundred seventy-eight restaurants, two hundred thirty-two tailors, and sixty-three radio repair shops, as well as two hundred ninety-seven doctors, seventy-four dentists, one hundred and two furniture stores, and fourteen loan offices. Hungrily our map devoured these statistics. With all the different markers in it, it began to look like a pin cushion.

While many of the things we discovered we already knew, it was both significant and depressing, both to students and to us teachers, to realize that a community which could support forty-one religious institutions and twenty-two political clubs could boast only a few open playgrounds for its children, three public halls, no neighborhood newspaper at all. . . .

At this time we had already started our campaign for a housing project in East Harlem and a new building for our school. But the legwork of our students showed that it was one thing to talk about modern housing projects such as those being launched in other parts of the city but another to overcome the many problems involved. The idea of compact units with thousands of families living in comfortable apartments, each with independent toilet and bath, was wonderful to contemplate and fight for. But what would happen to the dozens of little merchants in each block who would be dispossessed? Was no one to consider the five hundred and six candy store owners, the six hundred eighty-five grocers, the two hundred sixty-two barbers, most of whom had never known a home outside of East Harlem? Where would they go when the wrecking crews came in to wipe out six square blocks to make way for the new housing project? . . . We had to learn before we achieved the millennium. (pp. 205–206)

It is impressive, to me, that students learned so much about their local setting—that it served as a base for so much of their subject-matter learning. In the homogenization of our schools, what is most local is not critically examined—only serving to confirm the disconnectedness of the schools.

The connection of the school to the world came through in other ways at Benjamin Franklin Community High School. Covello noted:

Take the world of art, for instance. In too many city schools . . . the artwork produced by students used to depict a woodland scene, a landscape, or a seascape. Art, like poetry, was treated as something apart from the reality of daily living. We tried to get away from this at Franklin. There, art study tied in closely with our concern with the community. What many of the boys produced, as an expression of themselves, reflected their thoughts and ideas about the daily business of living in East Harlem.

Instead of a waterfall with a mill, a painting would show a mud-colored brick tenement with ugly fire escapes and laundry hanging on the roof; but on the front stoop, men in shirt sleeves caught a moment of sunlight. Instead of the surf and rock-bound coast of Maine, a charcoal sketch showed a dock on the East River and tugboats and kids swimming. It was vital art, and alive. In the midst of squalor it spoke the yearning for a better life.

The walls of our building were not decorated with reproductions of old masterpieces. We hung the best work of our students.

It made them proud and gave them an incentive to do better. (pp. 216–217)

Other examples grew from projects that related to community problems:

Each student was required to select a problem and follow it through. The group studying the problems of the slums was expected to make a personal investigation of actual slum conditions. The group studying problems of the "melting pot" had to ascertain through actual observation and personal investigation the difficulties presented in the adjustment of racial differences and animosities.

Each student had to turn in a midterm theme and a final term theme showing his personal reaction to the problem studied. These individual themes were something personal—essays, possibly stories, even verse, showing by the student's reactions to external stimuli what went on deep inside of him.

I have still in my possession one such theme given to me as a gift. It is a story in photographs done by a student named Hans Geissler. I remember him as a shy, blond lad always coming to class with a camera dangling from his shoulder. The photographs, bound into a book, show on the cover a Negro and a white man seated together in front of a fire made out of a few pieces of cardboard, trying to warm themselves, while the wretchedness of the slums spreads all around them. . . .

About the cover illustration itself he reported, "These two men earn their bare living by selling paper cartons which they pick up from refuse thrown out by grocery stores. It was a cold Sunday morning when this photograph was taken. The dying fire may well illustrate their dying souls, but do not let it be thought that they have given up hope or ambition. What little work they have to do, they do well. . . ."

The last photograph is a close-up—a portrait of a man's head. The mouth is firm, hard. The eyes sullen. The brow furrowed, as if the brain reaches for a balance between fury and despair. "The forgotten man—the refuse of the depression," wrote Hans. "His problems are our problems, because if we do not help him solve his, ours will never be solved." (pp. 217–218)

Teachers at Benjamin Franklin understood that students made larger commitments to topics they selected themselves, worked at over time, brought to a finished point. This meant a curriculum that was not overly prescriptive, that helped students learn what they needed to know in order to do what they wanted to do. Further, time was provided for students to do good work and to share their learning with others. As it is, students often don't complete much work in school that they truly honor.

As part of a research project that some colleagues and I have been working on, around a pedagogy of understanding, I have been asking students of all ages to describe those occasions in school when their learning was deeper than usual, when their personal intellectual engagement was particularly high, when they were conscious of achieving a higher level of understanding than usual. Interestingly, a large share of the learning experiences that matched these conditions occurred outside of school, though most could easily have occurred in schools. Of those that occurred in schools, that meant something special, the following circumstances were important:

- The students had a significant share of the responsibility for defining the content (selecting the *particular* subject to research, the *particular* biography to read, the *particular* play to present).
- There was time to wonder, work around the edges of the subject matter, find a *particular direction*, actually develop a personal commitment.
- Different forms of expression were permitted—even encouraged.
- There was an original product, something public—an idea, a point-of-view, an interpretation, a proposal, a paper, a presentation, a performance. Students gained in the process some form of "expertness."
- They actually did something—participated in a political action, wrote a letter to the editor of a newspaper or magazine, developed a newsletter, talked about their work with others.
- They made personal connections to the content, were called on to place themselves in the setting, and so forth. It was for them a "living experience." They were real scientists, not persons studying science.
- The content was connected to previous interests—in this regard, it had an ongoing quality. Additionally, it was related to the interests of others in the class.

- There was a sense that everything was not firm, predetermined, the results fully predictable.
- Students served as evaluators of their own work.

A curriculum concerned with student understanding, with moving students to a higher level of personal commitment, would take seriously these kinds of observations.

In recounting student projects—which came from students' own passions and meant something important to them—Covello was also making a statement about educational standards. He understood what many thoughtful teachers have also long understood, that students already possess standards as well as work toward new standards. That some students successfully researched land values in East Harlem and presented their work authoritatively meant that such work was possible and it was possible for others. Doing primary research on community issues became more and more commonplace. When the first student presented a documentary history with photographs as a base, such documentary histories became more common. The first literary review brought other literary reviews. The first set of biographies of East Harlem residents stimulated other biographies. High-quality work made visible, shared with other students and members of the community, was a catalyst at Benjamin Franklin for ever higher quality work.

This dynamic character of standards (Carini, 1994) must be made more central to current thought in schools. As it is, standards are being established externally and mostly in static language. They are not likely to encourage among students or teachers their best work.

◆ 1 2 ◆

Under Covello's watch, students always played responsible roles. While he recounts many such examples in his autobiography, one stands out for me. The occasion was a presentation by Fiorello LaGuardia, then president of the Board of Aldermen of New York, a popular Italian politician, well known in the East Harlem community. Vito Marcantonio, representing *Il Circolo Italiano*, was to offer a student speech and then introduce LaGuardia. Covello recounts:

It would be difficult for anyone to forget the startled faces of the students gathered at assembly that day when Marc stepped forward on the speaker's platform and said, "This morning I am going to talk about old-age pensions and social security. . . ."

In a few moments, there was complete silence in the auditorium as Marc's impassioned voice pressed the argument for providing for the old age of people who with their labor had helped to build America but who had never been able to earn more than enough to feed their children and pay for the clothes on their backs. He spoke passionately, eloquently—and, I know, sincerely. ". . . for, if it is true that government is of the people and for the people, then it is the duty of government to provide for those who, through no fault of their own, have been unable to provide for themselves. It is the social responsibility of every citizen to see that these laws for our older people are enacted."

The applause which followed as Marc backed away from the lectern convinced me more than ever that adolescents are far more capable of serious thought and understanding than they are given credit for being. . . .

LaGuardia shook Marc's hand, slapped him on the shoulder in a congratulatory gesture. Then, in his own inimitable way, he thrust out his chin and picked up the thread of Marc's speech and used it as the basis for his own talk. "Our neglected citizens. . . ." His audience howled.

Assembly that day was a huge success. . . . Most important of all, for LaGuardia and Marcantonio it was the beginning of an association and friendship which was to endure for many years. Almost as soon as he had finished law school, Marc went to work in LaGuardia's congressional campaigns in East Harlem. When LaGuardia was elected Mayor of New York in 1933, Marc was elected to replace him in Congress. (pp. 153–154)

We don't typically help our students assume responsible roles in our schools, gaining the kinds of experiences that enable them to be actively involved in their communities. We certainly don't commonly ask them to consider contemporary dilemmas and, after careful research, offer possible solutions.

Covello brought large numbers of students—first at DeWitt Clinton and then at Benjamin Franklin—into the community, believing that an education that included active service was essential. Service has rebounded in contemporary schools, but in most settings it is carefully measured, aimed more at the student and his or her growth than at the related local communities and their well-being. In the best of situations, service activities would have a more reciprocal quality.

Large numbers of Covello's students were involved in citizenship education work, many at La Casa del Popolo (the people's house), which was devoted to immigrant families. Covello was actively involved in programs there before he got students involved. Recognizing that there were not enough teachers to meet the demand for citizenship education, Covello turned the problem over to the students, stating:

> We can't expect much help from the outside. After all, these are our own people. If we don't help them, who will? Are we going to allow them to be robbed of their rights as Americans simply because we are too indifferent to teach them English and train them to pass the citizenship tests? (p. 155)

Challenged by Covello to do real work in the community, large numbers of students volunteered. As Covello notes, the students "turned out to be vigorous teachers" (p. 156) who brought large numbers of adults through the entire naturalization process. This was yet another venue for involving students in active citizenship, providing students a larger measure of responsibility, self-efficacy, an important place in an intergenerational world. It seems that our schools today are more rigidly age-segregated than ever before. We have children engaged mostly with children their own ages. That we have what many call "a youth culture problem" is one result.

In the 1960s, many schools, as part of their commitment to the civil rights revolution, got students involved in voter registration drives. Like Covello's activities around citizenship training, this was genuine service. And in many communities, students are involved in building projects related to senior citizens or to Habitat for Humanity. These, too, represent genuine service work. In settings in which community needs are a focus of study, service activities assume this more salutary quality.

Two other service-oriented, academically related projects that Covello made much of in his autobiography and other writings related to the work of the Playlot and the Health committees. The Playlot Committee, responding to community concerns about play spaces for young children, cleaned up several rubble-filled lots for conversion into playgrounds. Working with large numbers of school and community volunteers and a host of city agencies, the members of the Playlot Committee opened their first playground in 1937—the Franklin Play-

lot. The opening ceremony generated considerable enthusiasm. Covello writes of this effort:

> We had achieved what we felt should be one of the basic aims of
> education—improvement of community life, not merely through
> discussion but through a demonstration of school-community ac-
> tion. It is true that recreational problems are city problems and the
> responsibility for their solution rests to a great extent with city
> agencies. But the citizens must assume the final responsibility and
> the ability to assume the responsibility must be inculcated in the
> growing child. (p. 254)

One of the projects of the Health Committee related to sanitary
conditions in East Harlem, something the newspapers often commented on. Along with educational activities, the committee also pro-
moted block efforts to clean up neighborhoods, giving prizes to those
blocks that had done the most. Importantly, the committee also organized petition drives to gain higher-quality city services, arguing
that the city did not address sufficiently the needs of poorer communities. In regard to this sanitation work, Covello acknowledged that it
was hard to know how much good all the work did but he believed,
nonetheless, that such efforts to make the community better provided
an important educational experience equal to anything else that might
have been offered.

Feeling confident about students' taking part in authentic community tasks where they would have to be responsible persons seemed
natural to Covello. Currently, children and young people tend to describe their school learning as having very little to do with their lives beyond school. When students speak of the "remoteness" of school—*and
they do*—they are really talking about the lack of connection between
school and the world outside. They are essentially acknowledging what
Alfred North Whitehead (1929/1959) noted—that most of what is taught
in school is not about life "as it is known in the midst of living it."

Students see, for example, homelessness and poverty in the streets
around them; they know about immigration as they hear so many languages being spoken; they are aware of racial discord, community
violence, drugs, war, famine, and environmental degradation. That
schools do not explore such issues deeply, for the most part even ignoring them, reinforces for students that schools are about something
other than the realities of the world. This is unfortunate.

Further, the content of schools seldom relates to what people in a particular community are worried about or care deeply about. For example, the schools do not often make the historical and cultural roots or the economic and political structures of their local communities a focus of study. A community's storytellers, craftpersons, builders, day care and health providers, are not common visitors. The literature that is read has generally not been selected because it helps students assume a larger sense of responsibility for some aspect of the social good or makes it possible for them to engage a nonschool mentor more productively or assist a person in need. This disconnectedness trivializes much of what students are asked to learn.

We know all of this intuitively. While this knowledge causes many in schools to make occasional forays into the community—a walk to the park in relation to a science project, going to the local library so every student will get a library card, inviting in a couple of persons each year to share some aspect of their experience, having a cultural-awareness day related to the special ethnic origins of a dominant community group, having students go sporadically to a senior citizen center or read to children in a lower grade level—such efforts tend to be viewed as special events surrounding the *real* work of the school. This is the case even as teachers and their students often view these efforts as the *highlights* of the school year.

In relation to the foregoing, I am reminded of the project week organized recently by a Boston High School. Involving all the students and teachers, the week focused on the question: "Is Boston a livable city?" Students conducted a large number of interviews and surveys; visited cultural sites; read city and state crime, health, and environmental studies; and so forth. They concluded the week with various oral and written reports, what those in the school call "exhibitions of learning" and many at Harvard call "understanding performances." The intensity *was* very high. The students I worked with were sure they deserved a Harvard degree for their accomplishments of the week. It *was*, without question, the highlight of the year, causing many students to ask why this kind of intensive study around authentic issues could not be more the norm, the regular program, with what was the regular program moved to a special week. It seemed to me a reasonable question.

I believe we owe it to our young people to assure that they are deeply involved *with* their communities, that they leave the schools eager to take an active part in the political and cultural systems that surround them. Enlarging our vision of the school is, therefore, important. Covello understood this extremely well. He provides us many examples of how to proceed.

✦ 1 3 ✦

One of the currently popular educational mantras is the need "to hold high expectations." Another, closely related, is "every child can learn." Covello just had "faith" in his students. Actually, I like his simple statements better than the slogans we now use. He writes in regard to this faith in the students:

> Never in all my years of teaching have I said to a boy, "You can't do it." Who is there who can pretend to know the hidden capacities of another human being? I believe that more than often it is lack of faith on the part of adults which mars and even destroys the hopes of young people. (p. 204)

How many students have we all known who chose to go beyond what anyone expected of them? who decided at some point to do something they hadn't, for some reason, been able to do before? I remember a student who had been placed in mostly nonacademic courses in high school, who seemed unable to read and write beyond some very elementary level, who completed high school with mostly D-level grades, which many of his teachers suggested were "gifts." He was, however, an excellent athlete, in spite of a severely disabled hand/wrist. During the second semester of his senior year, he said to me that he wanted to go to college and continue wrestling. Having seen him compete as a wrestler, I had to acknowledge his extraordinary skill. I also knew that it wasn't possible to do what he could do as an athlete without a high degree of basic intelligence and strong will. Some tutors were acquired for him and a year later (a year past his graduation), he managed to score well enough on the ACT to get admitted to a university in spite of his academic record.

I didn't stay in touch with this young man. Some twelve years later, however, I received a long letter from him. The handwritten letter was fully legible, in standard English, grammatically perfect. There were many reminiscences about our relationship through his high school years, the lessons he had learned from me, how he chose to live his life differently than he might once have considered possible. He also discussed highlights of the years that had passed since I had last seen him: It had taken him five and a half years to complete his university degree; he had been very successful as a collegiate wrestler; he was married and had two children; he was finishing his sixth year of teaching and coaching; his wrestling team had just won its third consecutive state championship and his peers had selected him State Coach of the Year. Needless to say, perhaps, the tears flowed. I could tell hundreds of similar stories, as could Covello. We just can't make judgments about what is possible for young people.

Students related often how Covello opened doors for them, helped them cross boundaries that often seemed like mountains. One of his students in an interview spoke for many: "Pop [the name Covello acquired from his students] had a talent to make individuals sense their potential and to push them beyond what they might have been satisfied with. He encouraged me to aspire to be an architect not a draftsman" (Peebles, 1968, p. 152).

Myles Horton (1990/1998), of Highlander, spoke of the need to see others and the world with two eyes, one focusing on *what is* and the other on *what can be*, with both always being in view. Covello saw his students in these terms, the possibilities always present. So many of us see what is present as *all* there is, which means limitations come to dominate our outlook.

Covello knew that many students from East Harlem, poor, with few role models of high levels of academic achievement, couldn't always see themselves as physicians, lawyers, academics, stockbrokers, managers. They spoke more often about being nurses, clerks, technicians, or bookkeepers. Part of Covello's motivation for service activities was to get his students into contact with adults who were doing many different things. He constantly brought to his school settings people who came from similar backgrounds who were doing things in the world that might have seemed impossible.

His doctors' group was an example. In 1927, he organized all the Italian-American graduates of DeWitt Clinton who were physicians or were in medical school to provide free physical examinations for current DeWitt Clinton students. While this activity provided a health service that might not otherwise have been available, the larger purpose was motivational, a way of helping students see beyond what they understood as boundaries. His work organizing graduates who were in New York City colleges as tutors and big brothers served a similar purpose. What is interesting, as well, is that so many graduates of DeWitt Clinton were so well steeped in service commitments that they were willing to play this ongoing role with Covello and the school.

Stories abound of students who refer to Covello as the person who provided young people a boost, who helped them cross the boundaries that seemed to be all around them. The following accounts are examples:

> He filled a hero void for most of us, not a cowboy hero, not a blood and thunder hero, but a true hero. His dedication could show in his own quiet way. He wasn't direct about it, wasn't lecturing to us about it, but he was a real big brother and a real father. He filled that need for most of us boys who were either immigrant boys or second generation boys.

> I was anxious to quit school and he showed me the open doors through which it was possible to attain a high school education and also he was able to show me the light that was never shown us at home or in the neighborhood. In other words, he saw the potential which I could never see at the time, not at that age or with the environment we had.

> He never gave up on anyone, no matter how poorly a child did, or how much trouble a child was in, he was out there to salvage. He was a salvation worker more or less—to salvage that child, and he would see the parent or have the parent come to see him. The fact that he was able to talk to them, there was someone in this large high school who could talk Italian to the parents made a very nice relationship. . . . I think he made the boys there feel that he really cared. It was a personal involvement. The very fact that they called him Pop is a clear indication of this. (Peebles, 1968, pp. 134–135)

The idea of "opening doors" is important. A few years ago, at an activity honoring a former teacher/principal of Lansing Eastern High School, I talked with a former student—someone I began working with when he was nine or ten in a summer program. He was an outstanding athlete in high school, but at that time, African Americans were still not being aggressively recruited by the large Midwestern universities. Through the efforts of many of his coaches at the school, he entered one of the state's regional colleges. In our long conversation, catching up on almost forty years, he told me about his one-and-a-half years of college, his work, his ten children. He was very proud of the fact that eight of his ten children had baccalaureate degrees, a ninth was a senior in the university, and his tenth was finishing her last year of high school and was being heavily recruited as a basketball player. I was particularly impressed by his comment that "I didn't finish college, in fact I wasn't successful there, but those of you who helped me get there helped show me *how you go to college* and I learned at college what is really necessary to succeed. I was able to share *all* this with my children." In some respects this is a crossing boundaries story. But it also speaks to the matter of possibilities.

❖ 14 ❖

The struggle for a new high school in the East Harlem community had gone on in earnest during the 1931–1934 years. But what kind of school would it be? As the debate about a new high school in East Harlem ensued, it seemed that the board was willing to consider an industrial school but not an academic school. Covello's immediate response was:

> An Industrial High School in this community presumes to make trade workers of the boys who come there. We need a high school that is broader and better equipped to take care of the ambitions and life aims of all the boys, i.e., boys who want trade, and boys who want commercial or professional preparation. Such a general high school would also reflect its influence into the community and would be the center of civic improvement. (Peebles, 1968, p. 190).

This notion of providing for poor children something other than academic education has remained a serious problem almost to the present. It has, over the years, taken on many forms, the more recent being a heavy tracking system.

The announcement of a new high school in 1934 coincided with the election of Fiorello LaGuardia, an East Harlem resident, as mayor. While it was generally assumed that Covello, who had been the principal organizer of the drive for a high school in East Harlem, would be named principal, a prominent staff member of the school board, Fred Kuper, recalls his attempt to dissuade him from accepting that principalship.

> I said, "You are going to be a high school principal and you [are ready to] take a school in East Harlem or in Harlem. There is no decent building there and I know the general attitude of the administration at school headquarters." They didn't give a damn about it, and therefore, I said, "All you'll get is a cesspool. You'll

get some downtrodden kind of a building which should be de-
molished. . . . Then you'll try to get a new building and I have seen
one principal who broke his heart to get a new building and died
in the effort. . . . He finally got a building but before it was really
completed he was through. Now, the heart-breaking job of getting
a building for any high school is that there are so many and so
many demands. You'd be at the end of the line, and I would advise
you, we've just finished some new buildings such as Bay Side
High School, and other high schools, and, after all, with everybody
knowing the friendship and the regard which LaGuardia has for
you, you could take your pick." I never got spanked quite so well
as he spanked me that day. He stopped short, looked at me and he
said, "Fred, are you talking to me: I don't want just to be a high
school principal. I have a job, I'm head of a department and Rose
and I have sufficient income from that. We live modestly, I don't
need just more money and another job. East Harlem has been my
job. . . . If I don't get that school in East Harlem, I don't want the
principalship." (Peebles, 1968, pp. 205–206).

The principalship for Covello was not a "career move," a step toward Brooklyn (the site of power for the New York public schools) or
to one of the colleges or universities in New York City or elsewhere. It
was a continuation of his life's work in East Harlem. It meant doing on
an even larger scale, possibly, he hoped, with greater effect, what he
had been doing in DeWitt Clinton with increasing numbers of Italian-
American and Puerto Rican students and large numbers of families
and various service-oriented associations in the local community.
Of the challenge of the school, Covello noted:

Instead of working with one minority group, I would be in a position to work with many groups. It would provide a unique opportunity for us to test in a living situation the oft discussed idea that
it was possible for people of different origins, coming from many
countries with differences in language and customs to work together to improve community living; face such community problems as lessening group tensions and juvenile delinquency, better
housing and health facilities and a host of other community problems by creating a united front. (Peebles, 1968, p. 206)

John Dewey (1916) spoke of schools as centers for democratic education, having as a central purpose the formation of a democratic soci-

ety. Covello understood this more fully than did most American educators. He saw the Benjamin Franklin Community High School as the
epitome of Dewey's democratic conception, constructed around the
view that community well-being was an essential purpose. He wrote,
in relation to this tie between schools and their surrounding communities (which, at the time, as is the case today in many of our urban settings, were filled with immigrant families, living through a myriad of
cultural conflicts), that the schools "occupied a unique position"
(Covello, 1936, p. 1).

> It is the only social agency that has direct contact with practically
> every family within the community and the education law makes
> this contact with the family compulsory from the early childhood
> to the late adolescence of every boy and girl. This is important
> when one realizes that the public-school system functions in a
> city which has a population of close to seven million people, of
> whom one million two hundred thousand go to school. . . . To ac-
> complish [its mission on behalf of immigrants] it is necessary
> first to allay the distrust and the antagonism that have risen out
> of misunderstanding and indifference. Disruptive forces must be
> replaced with a spirit of friendliness and intelligent cooperation
> in the building of wholesome social and civic relationships. (p.
> 340)

To say that the schools should be community centers does not
mean that they were fulfilling such roles. He noted in this regard:

> Has the school really felt the life of the community pulsating be-
> yond its four walls? Has it made an attempt to realize the prob-
> lems and difficulties with which the immigrant neighborhood is
> faced? Has it answered the community call for help and its need
> and longing for guidance? To what extent has the school pene-
> trated into the community, analyzing, encouraging, and develop-
> ing its latent educational forces, and helping to counteract the
> forces of disorganization that apparently even the highly organ-
> ized society of today seems unable to curb even in the better or-
> dered communities? (p. 219)

How did Covello describe the aims of the Benjamin Franklin
Community High School? What did he believe should be the aims of
all schools? I outline below several of his definitions:

- The community-centered school is a school that reaches out into the community in order to make available to the community all of the resources of education.
- It implies an educational program based upon the principles of democracy in that it seeks to draw the community into conference with the school in order to determine the needs of individual students, the needs of the community as a whole, and the needs of the school, *in relation to* the community.
- The community-centered school endeavors to prepare its students for intelligent leadership and intelligent participation in community and national life by providing opportunities for leadership and participation while the student is yet in school.
- The community-centered school accepts responsibility for the social well-being of the community, as well as for the educational training of students committed to the care of the school.
- In carrying forward its program, the community-centered school can function successfully only if it be willing to become the friend and neighbor, as well as educational leader of the community. There must be understanding and cooperation between the school and the community before either can carry out his full responsibility in relation to the youth of the community.
- The program of the community-centered school, therefore, must be all-inclusive; it must be as broad as itself; it must be rooted in the human needs, the human aspirations, and the human capabilities of the individuals that comprise the community. (pp. 345–346)

This community-school conception is certainly rooted in democratic principles. Why is it so difficult to put such principles into practice? Our continuing task is to link communities and schools, to see them as integrally related, mutually dependent on one another.

The Community Advisory Council was the vehicle for coordinating the work of Benjamin Franklin as a community school. Covello wrote about its virtues as follows:

Our whole Community Advisory Council approach is predicated on the thesis that there should be a greater correlation between the neighborhood social agencies and the school. . . . Our teachers should know more about the educational work of the settlement houses and the settlement houses should know more about the social progress of the schools. (Peebles, 1968, p. 215)

A student participant in the Community Advisory Council wrote his own statement.

There was a time when the school was merely a place in which certain subjects were taught to children and that was all. That time is, I believe, past. The school is now the center of the community. From its position there radiate many channels of neighborhood activity. This activity, as carried on in Benjamin Franklin High School, is absolutely necessary. Especially is it necessary in a large city like New York, which contains so many communities, each with its own problems.

We . . . are striving to establish our school as a place where all may get together and discuss the problems peculiar to our own district. In order to do this, leaders in the community and institutions such as library heads, hospitals, social workers, welfare organizations and political leaders are asked to join our various community advisory groups. In such groups the student should certainly not be forgotten. He is often more acutely aware of neighborhood problems than are his elders. . . . The school might very well be a meeting ground where parent and child could get together. Very often the parent does not understand English which is all the more reason for the schools taking a hand. In Franklin we haven't a "Parent-Teachers Association," but a "Parent, Teachers and Friends" organization. Now among these friends might very well be included the parents' children. We shouldn't have open school "week" but rather open school year. This will come about naturally as the school interests itself in community affairs. (Peebles, 1968, pp. 215–216)

The struggle for low-cost housing in East Harlem was led by a student-community committee associated with the Benjamin Franklin Community High School. As was the case with virtually every community issue undertaken, study, research, and community education and participation were embedded activities. The housing drive began with research on various existing conceptions of urban housing, followed by model building and drawings (rooted in the research and developed within existing areas of East Harlem). These formed the basis for a large exhibition to educate the community.

At the same time, speculators were trying to buy up East River frontage for expensive apartment complexes. Covello notes:

To permit this would have been an injustice to the people of the community . . . we organized more meetings, held parades through the streets of East Harlem, distributed leaflets asking for the help of every man, woman and child in our efforts to obtain better housing for our people. We circulated hundreds of petitions addressed to the Mayor and the NY City Housing Authority. (pp. 219–229)

As it turned out, the community won a great victory, and engaged in a large community celebration, as funds were approved for low-rent housing adjacent to East River Drive. It became a model for additional efforts to acquire more housing for the community.

Getting a new high school building had many of the qualities of the work on housing. The larger struggle, in the end, revolved around the site. The students settled on the East River Drive site.

"Why shouldn't we have the most beautiful location for our school?" everyone asked.

The answer was that this site would probably cost more than any of the others. The students took matters into their own hands. Shortly after this, at a radio panel discussion, they had a chance to discuss this same question of site with Mayor LaGuardia. "The East River location is much more expensive," he said. "I'm afraid we'll have to settle for one of the others."

The spokesman for the student committee got up. "Mr. Mayor," he said, "our social-studies teachers arranged for us to make a study of land values. We checked the record and we found that according to the assessed valuation, the East River Drive site would actually cost less than any of the others."

Mayor LaGuardia seemed flustered for a moment. Then with the humor and poise characteristic of him, he said, "We'll discuss it after the program, boys."

In fact, after the radio program, the mayor had quite a talk with the students. . . . "If you're right," he said, wagging a pudgy finger, "and I believe you are, I will do everything possible to make this the site for the new school." (p. 228)

The school was opened in April 1942. Covello notes of the dedication ceremony:

War colored the entire ceremony that day. Mayor LaGuardia reminded the boys that whether or not the war ended before they could serve in it, they would face another war against dislocated conditions and that they had to bring themselves to realize the enormity of their responsibilities and prepare for them.

As I stood up on the platform of our magnificent auditorium, capable of seating thirteen hundred people, facing my students, my friends and neighbors of East Harlem, I could hardly speak. "To those of us who have lived and worked in this community for many years," I said, "this occasion marks the fulfillment of a long cherished dream-the dream of transforming dirt and ugliness into spaciousness and beauty, of bringing light into darkness. . . ."

In speaking about the program of the school, I added, "Fulfilling the ideal of Community Service to which it has been dedicated, the Benjamin Franklin High School will now operate on a round-the-clock program of use by all community organizations. Believing that a school building should be available to all the members of the community, all the time, the Board of Education has conferred a signal honor on Benjamin Franklin High School.

"By a special vote it has decreed that our building is to be open every hour of every day of the year. This means that we who live and work in East Harlem are free to use its magnificent resources at all times." (p. 230)

Currently, there is growing interest in keeping school buildings open beyond the regular school day and into the summer season. Given the fact that schools are the most common, most visible public facilities that exist in most communities, it seems wasteful to have them empty, unused for so much of the time.

An important feature of the Benjamin Franklin Community High School was the Wednesday Night Principal's Conference, which afforded an opportunity for community people, parents, and students to seek assistance, promote an idea for the school, or register a complaint. Covello was available each Wednesday from 6:00 to 10:00 P.M. As it turned out, many of the teachers also came. Covello indicated:

When we were not discussing school problems among ourselves, we interviewed parents and people of the community who sought our advice on everything from citizenship to childbirth.

It might be an Irish mother whose son had a fine voice, trying to find a way to further his musical education. Or an Italian woman with a black shawl tied over her head looking for her son who had not been home for a week. Or a father wanting his son to quit school, to go to work in his grocery store or shoe shop, and questioning our moral right to hold him there. Or a Puerto Rican couple with three children having difficulty with their landlord. Or a Jewish storekeeper complaining about the pranks played upon him by some of our boys.

We heard them all, talked to them in the language they understood, helped them when we could, referred them to the proper social agency, or just listened with an ache inside when we could do nothing at all. (p. 196)

Covello was happiest when the Benjamin Franklin School was serving the fullness of the community. He writes in regard to his Wednesday nights at the school:

Throughout the building, classes were in progress. I could sit in my office and listen happily to the hum of knowledge. Young men and adults who for one reason or another had been unable to graduate from day school were now completing their high school education at night. In other rooms immigrants of varying ages and nationalities struggled with the complexities of the English language, sometimes taught by their own sons, while still others prepared for citizenship tests. In the gymnasium a basketball game was in progress, as often as not involving two Jews, two Italians, three Negroes, two Puerto Ricans and a fellow named O'Reilly. In the library, the Parent-Teachers Association was holding a meeting, while from the auditorium might come the shrill sounds of an argument that meant the Community Advisory Council was in session. (pp. 197–198)

As Benjamin Franklin's Puerto Rican student population grew, Covello sought ways of learning more about the Puerto Rican experience. Naturally, he had to go to Puerto Rico to hear the fullness of the language, hear the music, see the landscape, see people at work and play.

I asked some of my Puerto Rican students at Franklin to give me letters of introduction to friends and relatives on the island. They gladly complied. In all, I delivered almost fifty letters, covering the one-hundred-mile-long island from one end to the other. It turned out to be a wonderful way of projecting myself into the lives and backgrounds of these people.

Most of the addresses were in and around the principal cities like San Juan, Ponce, and Mayaguez. With the possible exception of two or three families, all the letters I delivered were in the poorer sections of these cities.

No sooner did it become known that I was the schoolmaster of, for instance, Gerardo Vega, who was the son of Anna and Salvador Vega, who had left for New York several years before, than people would come pouring out of the houses on the street where the Vegas once lived to greet me . . . questions were fired at me from all sides concerning all the Puerto Ricans in New York. (pp. 262–263)

Was it easy to build a community school? To bring people together to forge a new education of power and consequence? In a reflection on his work, shortly before he died, Covello noted:

In the '30s my aim was to bring the community into the school, so that our youngsters might better grow into understanding and participating citizens. We developed a community advisory council, inviting representatives from education and religious organizations, foreign-born groups, social service agencies, civic groups, prominent citizens, business and professional groups, and municipal departments. But it wasn't easy to make these people understand that the school wanted them. They said, "What do you mean? That's *your* job. We have nothing to do with the school." And I answered, "Why, no, it's *our* job; we want you to become involved in the education of our children." (Covello, 1969, p. 17)

Yet participation grew. In all, twenty-two Community School Committees were organized. Each met at least once every two weeks. Participation of community members was exemplary. Moreover, the Community Education Adult Program, which began after 3:00 P.M. each day, became extremely popular. In the spring term of 1938, 1,700 adults were involved in programs from citizenship preparation to literature classes, language classes (Italian, English, Spanish), cultural studies, art, and dance. There were also social programs, the Friday evening dances being only one.

Covello sums up his lifelong commitments early in his autobiography as he describes his work after retirement.

As educational consultant in New York City to the Migration Division of the Department of Labor of the Commonwealth of Puerto Rico, I am trying to give the latest of our migrants—the Puerto Ricans—what I tried to give to the Italians and the Negroes, to the Irish and Germans, to the rest of the nationalities and races that make up that human mixture known as East Harlem: my time, my affection, and above all, my understanding. For only he who has suffered, directly or indirectly, the degrading insults of *wop* or *nigger* or *spick* or *mick* or *kike*—or whatever else the unwanted or newcomer to this land is called—can readily understand.

I have known all these things. I have known the hunger for food and the much greater hunger for knowledge. I have known fighting and stealing and the life of the back alleys and the city pavements, and also the life of the spirit at the mission house and the helping hand of some truly magnificent men and women. I have known all of these things, and if I had it to do over again, it is hard to say what change, if any, I would make. (pp. 1–2)

Leonard Covello lived a full life, a truly American life that began in Southern Italy and ended in East Harlem, working on behalf of others, seeing in the children, young people, and their families from this diverse community the wellspring of a more democratic America. He has provided a working model for those of us who still struggle with a vision of possibility, who understand that America needs the best our youth can provide, who continue to believe that our newest arrivals give promise for a better America. And he provided us a vision of what a school at the center of a community, being integral to a community's well-being, an important resource, a place where children and young people are understood to be genuine citizens, prepared to make ongoing contributions, can be like. We need to bring schools and communities together again, to reestablish the integration that makes of both something larger, that brings us closer to the democratic life that we need.

BIBLIOGRAPHY

In addition to the references used in the text, I have added to this bibliography some other texts I believe will be useful as companions.

Addams, J. (1910). *Twenty years at Hull House.* New York: Macmillan.
Buckley, J. (1986). *The turning key: Autobiography and the subjective impulse since 1800.* Cambridge, MA: Harvard University Press.

Carini, P. (1994). Dear Sister Bess: An essay on standards, judgment, and writing. *Assessing Writing, 1*(1), 29-65.

Cordasco, F. (1975). *Studies in Italian American social history: Essays in honor of Leonard Covello.* Totowa, NJ: Rowman and Littlefield.

Cotton, K. (1996). School size, school climate and student performance. *Close-up, #20.* Portland: Oregon: Northwest Educational Laboratory.

Covello, L. (1936, February). A high school and its immigrant community. *Journal of Educational Sociology, 9.*

Covello, L. (1943, January). A community centered school and the problems of housing. *Educational Forum, 7.*

Covello, L. (with Guido D'Agostino). (1958). *The heart is the teacher.* New York: McGraw-Hill

Covello, L. (1967/1943). *Social background of the Italo-American school child: A study of the Southern Italian social mores and their effect on the school situation in Italy and America.* Leiden: E. J. Brill.

Covello, L. (1969, January). Interview with Leonard Covello. *Urban Review, 3.*

Cubberley, E. (1909). *Changing conceptions of education.* Boston: Houghton Mifflin.

Davis, A. (1967). *Spearhead for reform: The social settlements and the Progressive movement, 1890-1914.* New York: Oxford University Press.

Denzer, E. and Wheelock, A. (1990). *Locked In/Locked Out: Tracking and Placement Practices in Boston Public Schools.* Boston: Massachusetts Advocacy Center.

Dewey, J. (1916). *Democracy and education.* New York: Macmillan.

Dewey, J., & Dewey, E. (1962/1915). *Schools of tomorrow.* New York: Dutton.

DuBois, W. E. B. (1920, July). Race intelligence. *The Crisis.*

DuBois, W. E. B. (1993/1903). *The souls of Black folk.* New York: Knopf.

Duckworth, E. (1996). *"The having of wonderful ideas" and other essays on teaching and learning* (2nd ed.). New York: Teachers College Press.

Freire, P. (1971). *Pedagogy of the oppressed.* New York: Herder and Herder.

Glazer, N., & Moynihan, D. (1971). *Beyond the melting pot.* Cambridge, MA: M.I.T. Press.

Greene, M. (1978). Wide-awakeness and the moral life. In M. Greene (Ed.), *Landscapes of learning* (pp. 42-52). New York: Teachers College Press.

Handlin, O. (1957). *Race and nationality in American life.* Boston: Beacon Press.

Hernstein, R., & Murray, C. (1996). *The bell curve: Intelligence and class structure in American life.* New York: Simon & Schuster.

Higham, J. (1955). *Strangers in the land: Patterns of American nativism.* New Brunswick, NJ: Rutgers University Press.

Horton, M. (with J. Kohl & H. Kohl). (1998). *The long haul: An autobiography.* New York: Teachers College Press. (Original work published 1990)

Kallen, H. (1924). *Culture and democracy in the United States.* New York: Boni and Liveright.

Kohl, H. (1967). *Thirty-six children.* New York: New American Library.

Lippman, W. (1922, October 15 and November 29; 1923, January 3). Series of articles on Testing, *New Republic.*

Lintelman, J. (1986). *The go-betweens: The lives of immigrant children.* Minneapolis: University Art Museum, University of Minnesota.

McClelland, D. (1973, January). Testing for competence rather than for "intelligence." *American Psychologist, 28* (1), 1-14.

Meier, D. (1996). *The power of their ideas.* Boston: Beacon Press.

Peebles, R. (1968). *Leonard Covello: A study of an immigrant's contribution to New York City.* New York: Arno Press.

Perrone, V., et al. (1981). *Secondary school students and employment.* Grand Forks, ND: Bureau of Educational Research, University of North Dakota.

Perrone, V. (1991). *A letter to teachers: reflections on schooling and the art of teaching.* San Francisco: Jossey-Bass.

Perrone, V. (1997). Reflections on teaching: Learning to teach and teaching to learn. *Teachers College Record, 98* (4), 637-653

Schafer, A. (1966). *Vito Marcantonio: Radical congressman.* Syracuse, NY: Syracuse University Press.

Tobier, A. (1988). *In Louis Armstrong's neighborhood.* New York: Queens College School-Community Collaboration Project.

Weldon, S. (1982). *Register of the Leonard Covello papers, 1907-1974.* Philadelphia: The Balch Institute for Ethnic Studies.

Whitehead, A.N. (1929 and 1959). *Aims of education.* New York: Macmillan.

Zangwill, I. (1909). *The melting-pot, drama in four acts.* New York: Macmillan

SELECTIONS FROM

The Heart Is the Teacher

BY LEONARD COVELLO
WITH GUIDO D'AGOSTINO

Forty-five years of my life I spent as a teacher in the New York City public schools. Twenty-two of these years I was principal of the Benjamin Franklin High School located in the East Harlem district of Manhattan Island.

In this long lifetime of teaching, I have learned much about the ways of immigrant peoples and their American-born children. I was an immigrant boy myself. I know what the American school can do to maintain family unity. I also know how the school can function as the integrating force in our democracy and in the molding of young citizens.

After half a century as teacher and principal, I retired—with the greatest regret. But I went right back to work with migrants. As educational consultant in New York City to the Migration Division of the Department of Labor of the Commonwealth of Puerto Rico, I am trying to give the latest of our migrants—the Puerto Ricans—what I tried to give to the Italians and the Negroes, to the Irish and Germans, to the rest of the nationalities and races that make up that human mixture known as East Harlem: my time, my affection, and above all, my understanding. For only he who has suffered, directly or indirectly, the degrading insults of *wop* or *nigger* or *spick* or *mick* or *kike*—or whatever else the unwanted or newcomer to this land is called—can readily understand.

I have known all of these things. I have known the hunger for food and the much greater hunger for knowledge. I have known fighting and stealing and the life of the back alleys and the city pavements, and also the life of the spirit at the mission house and the helping hand of some truly magnificent men and women. I have known all of these things, and if I had it to do over again, it is hard to say what change, if any, I would make.

From the window of my office at the Benjamin Franklin High School, I can see the East River Drive and the surging traffic of high-powered motor cars. It is Wednesday—the last Wednesday in August. For me it is the last Wednesday in school. It is the end of my life as a teacher in a public school. It seems impossible. I cannot quite convince myself that it is or could be the end. I had walked into a New York City classroom forty-five years ago. Life, for me, at that period, stretched interminably into the future. I always felt that my life in a school would go on and on until my last day.

I know that in September the now-empty classrooms and silent halls will once again feel the pulse of life as the boys—my boys—pour into every nook and corner of the building and take it over as they have done for so many, many Septembers—and I will not be there. It will seem strange not to stand again on the front steps and watch them as they converge upon the school, greet them as they come up the steps—children of the great metropolis: Negroes, whose parents migrated from the deep south; Italians, whose parents had forsaken the poverty-ridden villages of southern Italy; Puerto Ricans, from that stricken island in the Caribbean; Irish, Jews, Germans, Finns, and Swedes, migrants from every corner of the world, from near and distant places; people on the move, uprooted people, disinherited, seeking a new and better way of life, fleeing from lands where oppression and exploitation had been their daily lot, in search of the land that would give them the status and dignity of free men.

Once more the exuberance of my boys will fill the corridors. Their energy and vitality will fairly burst the seams of this great building as they pour in. I see them, the fair-haired and the dark, in the colorful array of their clothing and the pigmentation of their skin. How difficult it is to leave them!

I get up from my desk. Beyond is the East River, catching a brilliant reflection of sunlight. In this dazzling blur and in the pain within me, I see another land and another sun and the first of all those leave-takings which are part of life and, at the same time, a bit of death.

"Narduccio," my mother is saying, "come away from the window. Your father is gone now. We must wait. We must be patient until he calls for us and we can go to him in America."

All around is the dead pastel of an Italian landscape in the year 1891. And the solid masonry of walls that have withstood the centuries, as if the town had emerged from the mountain itself. The winding cobbled streets of the mountain town converge upon the *piazza* below. And the hot, humid wind from the south tortures the mind and can spell ruin for the peasant and his meager patch of land just outside the walls of Avigliano.

The town of Avigliano faced west, and it was westward that my father had gone, one more among the thousands upon thousands of southern Italians traveling to America in search of bread for his family. I was the oldest of three children, and already the idea of family and the sense of responsibility was taking hold of me.

"Why did he leave us? He said he was coming back."

My mother drew me away from the window. "These are the things men feel they must do. It is destiny. We cannot question it. It is God's will. We can only hope that in the end it will work out best for all of us."

I was still too young for her to explain the fever that had gripped my father—to explain that he had to go to America with the others. . . .

"You must watch for the butterfly," my mother said, trying to comfort me, "When a butterfly enters the window, then we will have news of your father, and it will be news that he is sending for us."

I remember how I caught butterflies and turned them loose in the house. My mother smiled and tried to pretend and play the game with me, but it was an empty smile which fooled no one. My father had troubles of his own in America. He sent what money he could, but he did not write very often. It was difficult for him to set words to paper, as it was with all our people in those days.

When someone returned from America to Avigliano it was a big event. "An *Americano* is here," people would say, and gather in the *piazza*, or square of the town, for a personal interview with this extraordinary Aviglianese who had ventured across so many thousand miles of ocean to a wonderful new world and come back again. Usually the *Americano* had a huge gold chain spread across his vest, at the end of which reposed some masterpiece of the watchmaker's art— tremendous in size. He spoke slowly and deliberately, as though his native Aviglianese dialect were now an effort for him, and his conversation was spiced with such phrases as *Nuova Yorka! La jobba! Lu bosso! Alò—gooda-by*. And we hung on his words. . . .

These were hard times for us. My mother, my two younger brothers, Raffaele and Michele, and I occupied one room in the house of my father's brother, Zio Canio. But we also spent a great deal of time in the home of my mother's brother, who was a priest—Giuseppe Genovese. Zio Prete, or Uncle Priest, we called him. As the oldest males in the

two families, Zio Canio and Zio Prete shared responsibility for our up-
bringing. It was their duty. However, all major decisions had to receive
the blessing of my paternal grandmother, Nonna Clementina—
matriarch by right and personality. As the first-born, I kept close to my
own mother—the place reserved for the oldest son in a southern Italian family.

During the day I went to school, and after school I worked in my
Uncle Canio's shoemaker shop. Then if there were a few moments to
spare I played. But play, in the town where I was born, was not a part
of life, as it is here in America. Life was difficult and exacting. From the
moment of birth you had to learn to assume your responsibility in the
life of the family. Everyone had to contribute to the work of the *paese*,
or town. Every hand was necessary. You had a purpose in living and
that was to work and be of service. Play was a thing that happened
sometimes in the process of being alive. There were no such things as
organized play activities or toys, except an occasional rag doll for a girl
child, and this was merely preparation for the more serious task of
raising a family.

I was born and grew up among the men who had fought in the
wars of Italian unification. My uncles, cousins, and other relatives related stories about Mazzini and Garibaldi and particularly about the
brigands who infested the region of Lucania—stories told around the
fireplace with just the light from the burning logs. Children listened to
their elders. We rarely ventured even a question and never offered a
comment, for that was the way to absorb knowledge and wisdom.
Duty was stressed. *"E il tuo dovere!"* "It is your duty!" It was your duty
to prepare yourself for a useful life.

There were many of us apprenticed in the shoemaker shop of Zio
Canio. We never received money, except a few pennies on festival
days. It would have been morally wrong to accept money to learn how
to work. And from the discipline of the work there was no escape. On
sunny days we would work outside the shop, learning how to soften
the leather by working it in water, how to use the awl, fasten a pig's
bristle at the end of the thread, and gradually how to shape the leather
and form the shoe. . . .

Poets have sung of the sunny skies of Italy and of laughter and
music and love. There were these things too. But poets seldom climbed
the mountains of southern Italy, where from December to March there
was snow and ice and bitter cold, and where fuel was scarce and
clothing expensive and children did not play because to play was "to
wear out shoes, undermine health, and waste time."

"The student must suffer to learn!" [Uncle Canio's ongoing message.]

A student from our town who was studying medicine in Naples had to give up school because family resources gave out. Loss of prestige and personal frustration were more than he could bear. He went out to the *camposanto*, or cemetery, on the outskirts of the town. Next morning they found him lying in the family plot with a bullet through his head. No one condemned this act. It was a matter of family honor.

To make ends meet, my mother rented a little cubbyhole on the *piazza*, where she sold small quantities of olive oil and bread and other staples. Sometimes she would make enough money for our own food, but more often we ate *acqua sale*, which was nothing more than hard bread soaked in boiling water with a little olive oil and salt added for flavor.

We never had breakfast at home. Some of the older men would take a small cup of black coffee and go to the shop. When I left for school, I took with me a piece of bread which my mother cut from an enormous Italian bread loaf—the portion depending on how much was available for the week—and an onion or a tomato when in season. Often we would share our food with some poorer classmate whose family was temporarily without bread.

In the winter a semblance of warmth filtered to us from the fireplace and from the charcoal fire in a brazier set on the platform at the teacher's feet. At stated times we would form a line, warm our hands, and then go back to our benches and continue our writing lesson. One of the requirements for school attendance was that each pupil bring daily to class one or two pieces of wood for the fire—and wood was scarce and hard to get.

School was from nine to eleven and from two to four in the afternoon. Sessions were short and attendance irregular. Our class was in an enormous square room near the *piazza* of the town, rented for the purpose. Light came only from several windows in the front. On dark or rainy days we neither read nor wrote. We recited individually or in small groups—mostly from memory. Our teacher, Salvatore Mecca, or Don Salvatore as we addressed him, was young, strong, vigorous, with a military bearing, a short-cropped mustache, and a Prussian haircut in the style of Umberto I, King of Italy.

As he entered the room we sprang up to attention from behind our crude benches.

"*Buon giorno, ragazzi!* Good morning, boys!"

"*Buon giorno*, Don Salvatore."

That was the signal for us to sit down again.

There were no girls in our school. Girls did not belong in the world of boys.

We had a book—one book, which our parents bought when we began school and which we used through several grades before passing it on to a younger brother. Even at that early age pupils often dropped out of school and never came back again. No one thought much about it, not even Maestro Mecca, who would blow his nose and comment, "Better thus. He is better suited for a hoe than a pen."

We learned the alphabet and spelling by singing it in unison:

b—a, ba; b—e, be; b—i, bi; b—o, bo; b—u, bu; ba—be—bi—bo—bu; ba—be—bi—bo—bu;

while the teacher strode around the room, the black ruler behind his back, apparently absorbed in his own thoughts.

Our one schoolbook contained all the elements of instruction, from arithmetic and geography to Roman and Italian history. There was one small blackboard, where the teacher would demonstrate penmanship and write down important dates and events. We learned mostly by rote, in limited areas, but thoroughly. It was our memory that was trained.

If we violated a school rule, physical punishment was meted out effectively, and that was only the beginning. The news of any infraction reached home quickly. There was no escape. We not only suffered cracks over the head for badly memorized lessons but also punishment on the knuckles from a square black ruler even for the way we held our pens. According to Don Salvatore, there was only one way in the world to hold a pen—his way. However, Salvatore Mecca was not a hard man. He was a teacher, teaching in the way that was expected of him, and to have taught differently would not have been understood or accepted either by the family or by the town.

As my uncle, Zio Prete, used to say, sitting in his enormous armchair, hearing my lesson and tapping his cane affectionately against my legs, "What comes easy is soon forgotten. What causes effort and torment is remembered all the days of one's life." . . .

As I look back upon my boyhood in Italy, I see many images and people, submerged and half forgotten, yet woven inextricably into the pattern of what was to be my life. I remember the huge, square room of my Uncle Canio's house where we used to spend time after supper and before going to bed, memorizing our lessons or listening to the stories of our elders—legends and terrifying ghost stories and particularly tales of the battles they had fought in the mountains of Lucania in that period when no man ventured outside the walls of the town without a musket on his shoulder.

We huddled about the fireplace for warmth in winter, but the solid masonry of the walls oozed dampness, so that it was never really possible to be comfortable. Closest by the fire, sitting straight in her chair, was Nonna Clementina, my paternal grandmother. Her gray hair, parted in the middle, was combed tight over her head and knotted. Her face was wrinkled and her hands bony and gnarled, and to us children she seemed as ageless as the mountains themselves and her position in the household just as secure. Even my Uncle Canio, stern-faced, bearded, and respected in the community, consulted her on all occasions and was swayed by her opinion. In our home she was the focal point around which all life revolved, even though now her vision was failing and it was difficult for her to get about. She knew all the herbs and remedies for every ailment. She could set a broken bone and apply the splints. I rarely saw a doctor in our home. And when there was a problem, she found the answer in the wisdom of her years and everyone listened to her. . . .

My mother was never very demonstrative with us children. This was characteristic of all our people once a child was beyond infancy. Her deep affection manifested itself in complete devotion to taking care of her family. She was of medium stature, dark-complexioned, with black hair combed straight back, and she never wore jewelry or ornaments of any kind except her marriage ring. She spoke in a low voice, and never became excited. No matter what happened, it was always as God had willed.

Neither my grandmother nor my mother could read or write, even though schooling was highly respected in our family and my mother's brother was a priest and my grandmother's father had been a lawyer. Schooling played no part in the lives of women. A man studied for the purpose of bettering himself—to become a notary, a druggist, a doctor, a lawyer, or an engineer. What was the purpose of schooling in the life of a woman? Would it help her bear a child? Raise a family? . . .

All we knew of our father was that he was living with the family of Vito Accurso—his boyhood companion—in New York, and that work was seasonal and life difficult. In fact, Uncle Canio often shook his head and said, "It is all very confusing. Everything is supposed to be so marvelous in America and money so plentiful, yet it takes so

ther the money for the passage." These were the
the people who remained behind could never un-

rco, or passage money, did arrive, it was received with
—gladness because the painful period of waiting was
ess because it meant going far away to a strange world
of no retu.... And sadness, too, because Nonna Clementina at about
this time had taken to bed, and it was obvious that the countless days
and nights of her years on this earth had run out and that she was
ready to die.

A week or so before we left Avigliano, she asked for me. I entered
her room, which had an ageless smell of lavender and mildew and the
olive oil with which she used to rub her hands. She was lying propped
against the pillow, her small wrinkled face almost lost beneath the
nightcap she wore. I leaned close to her and her fingers traced the outline of my face, as though to assure herself of what her ancient eyes
could no longer distinguish. Her voice was weak, almost a whisper,
but in her wisdom she had a final gift for me.

"Narduccio!" she said. "Narduccio *mio!* The gold you will find in
America will not be in the streets, as they say. It will be in the dreams
you will realize—in the golden dreams of the future."

❖   ❖   ❖

In the autumn of 1896, we arrived in America. As a boy of nine, the
arduous trip in an old freighter did not matter very much to me or to
my younger brothers. A child adapts to everything. It was the older
people who suffered, those uprooted human beings who faced the
shores of an unknown land with quaking hearts.

My mother had never been further from Avigliano than the chapel
just a few kilometers outside the town, where we went on the feast
days of *La Madonna del Carmine*. Suddenly she was forced to make a
long and painful trip from Avigliano to Naples, through interminable
mountain tunnels where choking black smoke and soot poured into
the railroad carriages. Then twenty days across four thousand miles of
ocean to New York.

When the sea threatened to engulf us, she did not scream and
carry on like the rest, but held us close with fear and torment locked in
her breast—voiceless, inarticulate. And when finally we saw the tow-
ering buildings and rode the screeching elevated train and saw the
long, unending streets of a metropolis that could easily swallow a

thousand Aviglianese towns, she accepted it all with the mute resignation of "*La volontà di Dio,*" while her heart longed for familiar scenes and the faces of loved ones and the security of a life she had forever left behind.

We spent two days at Ellis Island before my father was aware of our arrival. Two days and two nights we waited at this dreary place which for the immigrant was the entrance to America. Two days and two nights we waited, eating the food that was given us, sleeping on hard benches, while my mother hardly closed her eyes for fear of losing us in the confusion. . . .

Our first home in America was a tenement flat near the East River at 112th Street on the site of what is now Jefferson Park. The sunlight and fresh air of our mountain home in Lucania were replaced by four walls and people over and under and on all sides of us, until it seemed that humanity from all corners of the world had congregated in this section of New York City known as East Harlem.

The cobbled streets. The endless, monotonous rows of tenement buildings that shut out the sky. The traffic of wagons and carts and carriages and the clopping of horses' hoofs which struck sparks in the night. The smell of the river at ebb tide. The moaning of fog horns. The clanging of bells and the screeching of sirens as a fire broke out somewhere in the neighborhood. Dank hallways. Long flights of wooden stairs and the toilet in the hall. And the water, which to my mother was one of the great wonders of America—water with just the twist of a handle, and only a few paces from the kitchen. It took her a long time to get used to this luxury. Water and a few other conveniences were the compensations the New World had to offer.

"With the Aviglianese you are always safe," my father would say. "They are your countrymen, *paesani.* They will always stand by you."

The idea of family and clan was carried from Avigliano in southern Italy to East Harlem. From the River to First Avenue, 112th Street was the Aviglianese Colony in New York City and closest to us were the Accurso and Salvatore families. My father had lived with the Accursos during the six years he was trying to save enough for a little place to live and for the *l'umbarco.* . . . It was Carmela Accurso who made ready the tenement flat and arranged the welcoming party with relatives and friends to greet us upon our arrival. During this celebration my mother sat dazed, unable to realize that at last the torment of the trip was over and that here was America. It was Mrs. Accurso who put her arm comfortingly about my mother's shoulder and led her

away from the party and into the hall and showed her the water fau-
cet. "Courage! You will get used to it here. See! Isn't it wonderful how
the water comes out?"

Through her tears my mother managed a smile.

In all of her years in America, my mother never saw the inside of a
school. My father went only once, and that was when he took me and
my two younger brothers to *La Soupa Scuola* (the "Soup School"), as it
was called among the immigrants of my generation. We headed along
Second Avenue in the direction of 115th Street, my father walking in
front, holding the hands of my two brothers, while I followed along
with a boy of my own age, Vito Salvatore, whose family had arrived
from Avigliano seven years before.

My long European trousers had been replaced by the short knick-
ers of the time, and I wore black ribbed stockings and new American
shoes. To all outward appearances I was an American, except that I did
not speak a word of English. . . .

Already "yesterday" was taking on a new meaning. I was lonely. I
missed the mountains. I missed my friends at the shoemaker shop and
my uncles and the life I had always known. In the face of a strange and
uncertain future, Avigliano now loomed in a new and nostalgic light.
Even unpleasant remembrances had a fascination of their own. Who
had felt the blows of Don Salvatore Mecca could stand anything.

The Soup School was a three-story wooden building hemmed in
by two five-story tenements at 116th Street and Second Avenue. When
Vito pointed it out I experienced a shock. It appeared huge and impressive. I was ashamed to let him know that in Avigliano our school
consisted of only one room, poorly lighted and poorly heated, with
benches that hadn't been changed in fifty years. However, at this moment something really wonderful happened to take my thoughts from
the poverty of our life in Avigliano.

Before entering the school, my father led us into a little store close
at hand. There was a counter covered by glass and in it all manner and
kinds of sweets such as we had never seen before. "*Candi!*" my father
told us, grinning. "This is what is called *candi* in America."

"C-a-n-d-y!" know-it-all Vito repeated in my ear. . . .

The Soup School got its name from the fact that at noon-time a
bowl of soup was served to us with some white, soft bread that made
better spitballs than eating in comparison with substantial and solid
homemade bread to which I was accustomed. The school itself was
organized and maintained by the Female Guardian Society of Amer-

ica. Later on I found out that this Society was sponsored by wealthy people concerned about the immigrants and their children. How much this organization accomplished among immigrants in New York City would be difficult to estimate. But this I do know, that among the immigrants of my generation and even later *La Soupa Scuola* is still vivid in our boyhood memories.

Why we went to the Soup School instead of the regular elementary public school I have not the faintest idea, except that possibly the first Aviglianese to arrive in New York sent his child there and everyone else followed suit—and also possibly because in those days a bowl of soup was a bowl of soup. . . .

By the standards I had come to know and understand in Avigliano, the Soup School was not an unpleasant experience. I had been reared in a strict code of behavior, and this same strictness was the outstanding characteristic of the first of my American schools. Nor can I say, as I had indicated to Vito, that a blow from Mrs. Cutter ever had the lustiness of my old teacher, Don Salvatore Mecca. But what punishment lacked in power, it gained by the exacting personality of our principal.

Middle-aged, stockily built, gray hair parted in the middle, Mrs. Cutter lived up to everything my cousin Vito had said about her and much more. Attached to an immaculate white waist by a black ribbon, her pince-nez fell from her nose and dangled in moments of anger. She moved about the corridors and classrooms of the Soup School ever alert and ready to strike at any infringement of school regulations.

I was sitting in class trying to memorize and pronounce words written on the blackboard—words which had absolutely no meaning to me. It seldom seemed to occur to our teachers that explanations were necessary.

"B-U-T-T-E-R—butter—butter," I sing-songed with the rest of the class, learning as always by rote, learning things which often I didn't understand but which had a way of sticking in my mind.

Softly the door opened and Mrs. Cutter entered the classroom. For a large and heavy-set woman she moved quickly, without making any noise. We were not supposed to notice or even pretend we had seen her as she slowly made her way between the desks and straight-backed benches. "B-U-T-T-E-R," I intoned. She was behind me now. I could feel her presence hovering over me. I did not dare take my eyes from the blackboard. I had done nothing and could conceive of no possible reason for an attack, but with Mrs. Cutter this held no significance. She carried a short bamboo switch. On her finger she wore a heavy gold wedding ring. For an instant I thought she was going to pass me by and then suddenly her clenched fist with the ring came down on my head.

I had been trained to show no emotion in the face of punishment, but this was too much. However, before I had time to react to the indignity of this assault, an amazing thing happened. Realizing that she had hurt me unjustly, Mrs. Cutter's whole manner changed. A look of concern came into her eyes. She took hold of my arm, uttering conciliatory words which I did not understand. Later Vito explained to me that she was saying, "I'm sorry. I didn't mean it. Sit down now and be a good boy!"

Every day before receiving our bowl of soup we recited the Lord's Prayer. I had no inkling of what the words meant. I knew only that I was expected to bow my head. I looked around to see what was going on. Swift and simple, the teacher's blackboard pointer brought the idea home to me. I never batted an eyelash after that.

I learned arithmetic and penmanship and spelling—every misspelled word written ten times or more, traced painfully and carefully in my blankbook. I do not know how many times I wrote "I must not talk." In this same way I learned how to read in English, learned geography and grammar, the states of the Union and all the capital cities— and memory gems—choice bits of poetry and sayings. Most learning was done in unison. You recited to the teacher standing at attention. Chorus work. Repetition. Repetition until the things you learned beat in your brain even at night when you were falling asleep. . . .

Silence! Silence! Silence! This was the characteristic feature of our existence at the Soup School. You never made an unnecessary noise or said an unnecessary word. Outside in the hall we lined up by size, girls in one line and boys in another, without uttering a sound. Eyes front and at attention. Lord help you if you broke the rule of silence. I can still see a distant relative of mine, a girl named Miluzza, who could never stop talking, standing in a corner behind Mrs. Cutter throughout an entire assembly with a spring-type clothespin fastened to her lower lip as punishment. Uncowed, defiant—Miluzza with that clothespin dangling from her lip. . . .

❖   ❖   ❖

My father worked as general handyman in a German tavern or café on 22nd Street. Downstairs there were bowling alleys, and during the winter he was kept pretty busy setting up pins along with his other work, but in summer business slackened and he was often without work for weeks at a time. When he did work he made seven or eight dollars a week and extra tips. But work or no work, money in our house was scarce. My mother kept saying, "What are we going to do?" and my father would always answer, "What can I do? If there is no work there is no work. You'll have to do the best you can."

It was a curious fatalistic attitude among our people in America that while they deplored their economic situation they seldom tried hard to do anything about it. Generations of hardship were behind them. Life was such. "*La volontà di Dio!*" For them the pattern could never change, though it might, perhaps, for their children.

Our kitchen table was covered by an oilcloth with a picture of Christopher Columbus first setting foot on American soil. It was the familiar scene of Columbus grasping the flag of Spain, surrounded by his men, with Indians crowding around. More than once my father glared at this oilcloth and poured a malediction on Columbus and his great discovery.

One day I came home from the Soup School with a report card for my father to sign. It was during one of these particularly bleak periods. I remember that my friend Vito Salvatore happened to be there, and Mary Accurso had stopped in for a moment to see my mother. With a weary expression my father glanced over the marks on the report card and was about to sign it. However, he paused with the pen in his hand.

"What is this?" he said. "Leonard Covello! What happened to the *i* in Coviello?"

My mother paused in her mending. Vito and I just looked at each other.

"Well?" my father insisted.

"Maybe the teacher just forgot to put it in," Mary suggested. "It can happen." She was going to high school now and spoke with an air of authority, and people always listened to her. This time, however, my father didn't even hear her.

"From Leonardo to Leonard I can follow," he said, "a perfectly natural process. In America anything can happen and does happen. But you don't change a family name. A name is a name. What happened to the *i*?"

"Mrs. Cutter took it out," I explained. "Every time she pronounced Coviello it came out Covello. So she took out the *i*. That way it's easier for everybody."

My father thumped Columbus on the head with his fist. "And what has this Mrs. Cutter got to do with my name?"

"What difference does it make?" I said. "It's more American. The *i* doesn't help anything." It was one of the very few times that I dared oppose my father. But even at that age I was beginning to feel that anything that made a name less foreign was an improvement.

Vito came to my rescue. "My name is Victor—Vic. That's what everybody calls me now."

"Vica. Sticka. Nicka. You crazy in the head!" my father yelled at him.

For a moment my father sat there, bitter rebellion building in him. Then with a shrug of resignation, he signed the report card and shoved it over to me. My mother now suddenly entered the argument. "How is it possible to do this to a name? Why did you sign the card? Narduccio, you will have to tell your teacher that a name cannot be changed just like that. . . ."

"Mamma, you don't understand."

"What is there to understand? A person's life and his honor is in his name. He never changes it. A name is not a shirt or a piece of underwear."

My father got up from the table, lighted the twisted stump of a Toscano cigar and moved out of the argument. "Honor!" he muttered to himself.

"You must explain this to your teacher," my mother insisted. "It was a mistake. She will know. She will not let it happen again. You will see."

"It was no mistake. On purpose. The *i* is out and Mrs. Cutter made it Covello. You just don't understand!"

"Will you stop saying that!" my mother insisted. "I don't understand. I don't understand. What is there to understand? Now that you have become Americanized you understand everything and I understand nothing."

With her in this mood I dared make no answer. Mary went over and put her hand on my mother's shoulder. I beckoned to Vito and together we walked out of the flat and downstairs into the street.

"She just doesn't understand," I kept saying.

"I'm gonna take the *e* off the end of my name and make it just Salvator," Vito said. "After all, we're not in Italy now."

Vito and I were standing dejectedly under the gas light on the corner, watching the lamplighter moving from post to post along the cobblestone street and then disappearing around the corner on First Avenue. Somehow or other the joy of childhood had seeped out of our lives. We were only boys, but a sadness that we could not explain pressed down upon us. Mary came and joined us. She had a book under her arm. She stood there for a moment, while her dark eyes surveyed us questioningly.

"But they don't understand!" I insisted.

Mary smiled. "Maybe some day, you will realize that *you* are the one who does not understand."

At what I nostalgically and possessively call *my* school—the Benjamin Franklin High School in East Harlem—there is a gold-medal award given at each graduation to the student who has been of greatest service to his school and his community. This is called the Anna C. Ruddy Memorial Award, and it commemorates a woman who, though not very well known to the outside world, was a tremendous influence in East Harlem during a lifetime devoted to the cause of the recently arrived immigrant and his children.

Miss Ruddy was the daughter of a Canadian pioneer from Ulster County, the Protestant stronghold in North Ireland. She came to East Harlem from Canada about 1890 to do missionary work among the Italians—a job for which she prepared herself by learning how to speak and read our language. She had no money. At first she had very little help of any kind, only an overwhelming desire to bring some measure of hope into the dinginess of the immigrant's very crowded tenement life.

Miss Ruddy preached the teachings of Christ. That she was Protestant did not make any difference to us. In general, our fathers looked upon religion through half-closed eyes while the women, with endless household chores and children to look after, found little time for regular church worship. The younger people were left pretty much to make decisions for themselves. . . .

Many years of my life were spent under the influence of Miss Ruddy and the Home Garden, as her little mission was called. Yet, to catalog or classify it exactly is as difficult as it is to describe the unusual character of the woman who was its head. There was Sunday School and Bible reading—Miss Ruddy standing there, tall and imposing, her auburn hair swirling over her head and catching the sunlight which came through the windows of the small brownstone building which she had converted into a haven for the Italian children and young people of the neighborhood. She wore immaculately laundered blouses which buttoned close about her throat and a gold cross suspended by a fine gold chain—her only adornment. She read the Bible with the book settled loosely in the palm of her left hand, talking in a low, softly modulated voice, reading mostly from memory and only occasionally glancing down to reassure herself.

What meaning could Biblical verses and quotations have for the children of the slums of East Harlem? Who would listen to language that was like the ripple of water when in our ears rang the madness of the elevated trains and the raucous bellowing of Casey the cop above the cries of the fish mongers and fruit and vegetable peddlers as he chased us down the street? . . .

Away from the Home Garden we fought the Second Avenue gang with rocks and tin cans and used garbage-can covers for shields. We scavenged the dumps and the river front for anything we could sell to make a penny. We had a hideout under the tenement rubble where we played cops and robbers and took the fruit and sweet potatoes stolen from the pushcarts to cook in our "mickey cans." But at the same time we spent Sunday afternoon and several nights a week at the Home Garden with Miss Ruddy, where we formed another club called the Boys' Club. We read books, put on plays, sang songs. There was nothing strange about this duality, although it may seem so to people who have never been poor or lived in crowded big-city slums. . . .

❖   ❖   ❖

In Avigliano there were times when there was no food in the house. Then we bolted the door and rattled kitchen utensils and dishes to give the impression to our close neighbors that the noonday meal was going on as usual. After the *siesta* everyone went about his customary tasks and the outside world never knew exactly how it was with us. The intimate things of family life remained sealed within the family, and we created for ourselves a reserve both as individuals and as a group.

In America it was not much different. Our people had the worst possible jobs—jobs that paid little and were very uncertain. A stonemason worked ten hours a day for a dollar and a quarter—if there was work. When there was snow or rain or ice there was no work at all. During slack periods men just hung around the house or played *boccie* down in the vacant lot or played cards in the kitchen or in the café. They did not talk about their troubles, but their games did not have the usual gusto. The children especially could sense their feeling of helplessness in this land which offered little more than strangeness and hardship.

My mother lived in constant fear from the uncertainty of life. As the eldest child, I had been close to her in Avigliano. I was still closer to her here in America. There were now four boys in our family and my mother was expecting another child. I had to earn money somehow while I was going to school.

Miss Ruddy came to our assistance. . . . [She sent me to] Mr. Griffin, [who] owned a large bakery shop on 112th Street and Fifth Avenue. . . .

"You're not much for size or weight," he said. "It's hard work, running around delivering orders early in the morning. And it's an all-year-around job—six days a week, except the Sabbath. People want their bread when they wake up. Five o'clock we begin. If you're willing, it's a dollar seventy-five a week with a cup of coffee and a roll thrown in to perk you up before you start working. You begin Monday."

"I'll be here, sir," I said.

He laughed and grabbed a loaf of bread and thrust it under my arm. "Here, fatten yourself up a little. I'll see you on Monday."

I literally leapt from his office in my excitement. I ran home to tell my mother and father that I had found a job and was ready to do my share in supporting the family. My mother put her hand on my shoulder. My father said, "Good. You are becoming a man now. You have grown up." I was only twelve, but I could feel that he was proud of me. And I was proud of myself because I had reached the age where I could do more than scrub floors and wash windows and look after my baby brothers. I could earn money and stand on my own two feet and help keep the family together, as I had been taught practically from the time I was born was my responsibility.

At four-thirty every morning I walked rapidly over to Fifth Avenue and 112th Street to the bakery shop. There the day's orders were waiting for me to put into bags for delivery. After a hurried cup of coffee and milk and a couple of rolls, I started out pulling a little wagon that I had constructed out of an old packing crate and baby carriage wheels.

Servicing the private houses was not so bad where there were only a few steps to climb. However, the apartment houses were quite different. The cellars were dark and I had to grope along, banging into walls, stepping on cats, hearing rats scurry out of my way, and always keeping a wary eye for janitors' dogs. Sometimes, in the beginning I carried a lantern, but this was awkward with the bags of bread, so I had to learn to make my way through the darkness in and out of serpentine alleys to the dumbwaiters where the coarse rope cut my hands as I whistled to faceless customers who lived somewhere high up in the air like inhabitants of another planet.

It was rush, rush, rush, back and forth from the bakery until all the orders were delivered. Then I had to run home and get ready for school. For this work I received one dollar and seventy-five cents a week. It was not very much but it helped a great deal in days when meat was twelve cents a pound and milk six cents a quart. Thus when I was twelve, work became an inseparable part of life. . . .

This was the beginning of my work years—jobs after school and during summer vacation to help the family and in order to be able to continue in school. Next I worked for several summers in a baking-powder factory downtown on Barclay Street, passing the bakery delivery job to my younger brother Ralph. The hours at the factory were from seven-thirty in the morning until six at night and from eight until three on Saturdays. The wages were three dollars, out of which came sixty cents a week for carfare and sixty cents a week for lunch. This left me with only one dollar and twenty cents to take home to my mother. But every penny counted and helped to keep us going.

Mrs. Cutter and the Soup School were behind me now, in time if not in memory. I was going to Public School 83 on 110th Street between Second and Third Avenues. What an impressive school that was to me! Five stories high. Hundreds of boys. Halls. Regular classrooms. And a teacher by the name of Miss Sayles who gave me twenty-five cents a week to run up to her home, a brownstone building at 116th Street and Lexington Avenue, to bring back her lunch.

Once a week the huge rolling doors which formed the classrooms were rolled back and we marched into assembly. As at the Soup School, everything was done in silence, in unison, and at attention. From a side door Mr. Casey, the principal, would emerge—bearded, impressive, wearing a black skull cap, stiff white collar and black tie, and a long, loose black coat with white laundered cuffs which stuck out from his coat sleeves. There was the usual flag salute and the Bible reading. Mr. Casey swallowed his words and I could never understand what he was saying, except one favorite expression, "Make a joyful noise unto the Lord!" This completely baffled me because everywhere, in the classrooms, in the halls, on the stairs, strict silence was the rule. . . .

The constant drilling and the pressure of memorizing, the homework, and detention after school raised havoc with many students. For me, this type of discipline seemed merely the continuation of my training in Italy. I wanted to go to school. School meant books and reading and an escape from the world of drudgery which dulled the mind and wore out the body and brought meager returns. I had seen it often with my father and his friends when they came home at night tired and dispirited.

"Nardo," my father repeated again and again. "In me you see a dog's life. Go to school. Even if it kills you. With the pen and with books you have the chance to live like a man and not like a beast of burden."

I was seldom absent from school and never late. Geography and history I mastered easily. I memorized with facility. I more than held my own in spelling and widened my English vocabulary by working diligently at the daily exercises and homework which the teacher called "meaning and use." This expression baffled me for a long time. We used to walk along the street, saying, "Hey, I gotta go home and study 'mean 'n yourself'!" I did not worry about what the expression meant. I simply learned how to do it. The exercise involved a dictionary and a speller. We had to take five or six words from the speller, hunt for them in the dictionary, and then write a sentence illustrating their use.

Spelling bees were common in those days. The speller was graded with such words as "Mississippi" and "isthmus" in the lower classes and topped with words like "obliquity" and "Aix-la-Chapelle" and "aberration" and "capstone" in the upper class.

We memorized suffixes and prefixes, Latin and Greek roots, and we were required to give the meanings of words as they are used as well as their etymological meanings. Also each group of words had to be illustrated with "promiscuous examples." According to modern methods and educational theories, it was rough fare. But it had its values. It may not have been the best way to train the mind, but it did teach you to concentrate on mastering difficult jobs. . . .

During the last year of grade school, we had a period of German on Friday afternoon [with] Professor Hoffstadter, the German teacher. . . . For us it was the end of the week, and we waited impatiently to be off and away from school. . . . There was only the desire to get it over with as quickly as possible.

"You are a rambunctious bunch of bums!" [the professor] would shout, his beard sticking straight out at us like the point of a rapier. We had no notion of what he was saying but the sound delighted us. "Rambunctious bums!" we yelled to each other. One boy, I remember, was so amused by the sound of German that he leapt out of his seat and into the aisle, holding his belly, convulsed with laughter, while poor Hoffstadter blustered and turned red in the face.

When I graduated and went to Morris High School I again found German on my school program. Who put it there I never knew. At that time I did not know that I could have chosen Latin or French. I just accepted the fact that I had to take German and that was that. Nor did my parents or the parents of other students question the choice. No one said, "If the German language is taught in the schools, why not Italian?". . .

Now I was living what seemed like fragmentary existences in different worlds. There was my life with my family and Aviglianese neighbors. My life on the streets of East Harlem. My life at the Home Garden with Miss Ruddy. Life at the local public school. Life at whatever job I happened to have. Life in the wonder-world of books. There seemed to be no connection, one with the other; it was like turning different faucets on and off. Yet I was happy.

❖   ❖   ❖

When finally, after much delay, work on Jefferson Park was begun, those of us of the Aviglianese colony moved to tenements several blocks away. Instead of kerosene lamps, we now had gas light and a gas stove and a meter which kept us constantly scurrying for quarters. In the middle of a meal or at night while I was reading, the gas would lower under a boiling pot of spaghetti or the light would dim, and the meter would have to be fed. My father said it was like having an extra mouth in the family.

Instead of one toilet, there were now two toilets on each floor, serving four families. It was a definite improvement over our first home in America, but it also meant more rent to pay. And there were more mouths to feed and more clothing to buy, because now there were five of us children. The youngest, my sister Clementina, had just been born. In the end we were not much better off.

My mother was always tired now. We helped her as much as we could but she never seemed to get caught up with her work. There were times when she would sit with her hands folded in her lap, an air of weariness upon her. She lost all desire to go out into the street or to see anything new, as if just keeping alive was problem enough in itself.

Often Mary would say to her, "It is beautiful in the park now—grass, trees, flowers. You can sit in the sun on the new green benches."

My mother would only smile and perhaps touch Mary's hand in a gentle caress. "Run along. Today, I cannot. Tomorrow. Tomorrow when I will have more time. . . ."

Povera Mamma! The time she waited for was fast running out.

I remember in those days how we used all our resources to keep our parents away from school—particularly our mothers, because they did not speak English and still dressed in the European way with the inevitable shawl. We didn't want these embarrassing "differences" paraded before our teachers.

But the circle was widening. At first there were only Italians and Americans. The distinctions began as we from Avigliano started to differentiate between Aviglianesi, Neapolitans, Calabrians, and Sicilians. Then we came in contact with the Irish and the Germans and the Jews and the other nationalities outside the immediate borders of the Italian community. Our knowledge of the world—and, I'm afraid, our prejudices—spread out to embrace the enlarging borders of our experience. . . .

Whatever problems we had at school or in the street, we never took up with our parents. These were our personal problems, to be shared only by companions who knew and were conditioned by the same experiences. How could parents understand? Parents belonged in one of the many separate watertight compartments of the many lives we lived in those days.

This fear of ridicule, constant with us of foreign birth, was further aggravated when we went to Morris High School, which was coeducational and where practically all the girls came from a wealthier and older environment. We were not used to girls, and having to associate with them filled us with uneasiness. When we went anywhere or did anything, it was always with boys. This was the way we had been raised. In Italian families, practically from infancy, the girls are always separated from the boys.

That first day, four of us from East Harlem walked over to the annex in the Bronx where we were supposed to report to a special room. We found the room all right, but when we approached and saw some girls standing in the doorway, we drew back. "Girls!"

We went outside again. "Say," I said to Emil Panevino, one of my group, "did you know there were girls in this school?"

"No one said anything to me about girls."

"And American girls, too," my friend Victor commented.

"What are we going to do? "

We stood there huddled together, trying to gather enough courage to go back inside, when a gruff male voice said to us, "What's the matter with you boys? What are you standing there for? Don't you belong in school?"

At Morris High the pressure of work and study was much heavier, but the greatest obstacle was to establish any feeling of identity with these new students. They came from better homes in better sections of New York, and they possessed greater self-assurance—particularly the girls. Also they were well dressed and had spending money. They had a social life which we did not share and little gatherings to which we were not invited. In fact, we did not want to be invited for fear that in some way we might have to reciprocate. We did not want them to see our homes and our parents and how we lived. The circle widened only in the sense that we were thrown into contact with a larger community. We still kept very close to our own little East Harlem group.

Another thing which astounded me in those early days of high school was the tremendous emphasis placed on sports. The greatest prestige did not come to those who got the highest marks but to the athletes. They were the leaders. How many times I wondered what my uncle Zio Prete would have thought of such frivolity.

At first I was hesitant about taking part in athletics or striving to make one of the school teams. It seemed a strange way to spend one's time and energies—at play! Yet greater than all else was the desire to excel in the accepted way, to show that you were just as good as the next fellow no matter what the difference socially. Growing up in the rough-and-tumble life of East Harlem had given me certain physical advantages. The test came during a school-wide chinning contest. I was small but wiry. My arms were strong from pulling dumbwaiter ropes. I placed second in the entire school. This spurred me on to make one of the school teams so that I could proudly display the school emblem, a huge maroon "M" on a white sweater.

The excitement about the chinning contest was more than I could keep to myself. I had to tell the family about it, and it happened to be one of those rare nights when my father was home for supper. To the delight of my younger brothers, I explained the mechanics of chinning. My mother and father listened with interest for a few minutes. They looked at each other. The expression on my father's face changed from mild bewilderment to utter bafflement as I continued. I realized that I had made a tactical blunder but there was nothing I could do about it. Finally I blurted, "I was second! Second best in the whole school! That's something!"

My father threw down his napkin and pushed away from the table. He paced across the room gripping the back of his head. "There is hardly enough to eat in the house. We kill ourselves. We work so that he can have some future—and he spends his time at school playing!"

"It is not play! " I argued. "It is part of the school work. We have to do it." This only made my father angrier, and now my mother was upset.

"Then stop school and go to work. You do not have to waste money and time to be a strong man. A jackass is strong and he never went to school. The ditch-digger is strong. The man who cleans the sewers. Only they get paid for being strong while you get nothing. . . ."

It was no use. I should have known better. It was one of those times when ordinarily I would have resorted to the old standby, "You will never understand." Instead I said nothing, simply grabbed my school books and walked out of the flat. . . .

The threat to quit school that I had expressed to Mary in a moment of anger became a reality. At the end of my third year at Morris I decided to leave, and neither Mary nor the entreaties of Miss Ruddy could make me change my mind. The decision was solely my own, and I arrived at it one night after hours of wandering about the streets in the rain. Eventually a policeman, seeing me drenched and standing under a gas light, sent me home.

Whatever I could earn after school was not enough, despite the fact that my father was working and my two younger brothers were also contributing. The helpless attitude of my mother, the despair always in her eyes, her failing health, the medicines and the necessities we could not afford, were more than I could bear. I had to take a full-time job.

Where was I getting in school? I argued with myself. What was I going to become and how was school helping me? I was old enough now to work as a man. I had to work. In work I might be able to find the answer.

My parents were by this time so far removed from my multitudinous worlds that they no longer questioned my decisions. If I wanted to leave school now it was my own affair. No one would interfere, especially if it was to help the family. As always, the family came before other considerations. . . .

❖   ❖   ❖

[In the year out of school] I loaded and unloaded crates for a company that manufactured brassware on Murray Street in downtown Manhattan. From the street level the crates were hauled off the horse-drawn wagons and up to the second story by means of a hand winch which it was my job to operate for five dollars a week, including Saturdays. The first couple of days my hands became so sore and blistered that at night I could hardly open them, and my mother made me soak them in warm salt water.

We sat there together in the kitchen, the basin in her lap and my hands in the basin, and we didn't say much, but all the time I knew what she was thinking. She was thinking that I was a man now like my father and the others. I was working as they were working. Perhaps she was thinking that if I had stayed in school it might have been different. She looked at my hands and shook her head, saying *"Figlio mio!"*

The money I earned helped to make things a little easier at home. But the compensations were not nearly so great as I thought they would be. The things I had learned at the Home Garden kept running through my mind. "Man does not live by bread alone. . ." What else, then? I had tried living without bread for a while and see how far I had gotten. I stayed at home nights and Sundays. I borrowed books from the Aguilar Library and slept near the window so that in the morning, with the first rays of light, I could prop myself up on one elbow and read without disturbing my two brothers who were in the same bed.

I was restless, brooding. I hated the job and the winch and the packing cases and my callused hands, because I could see nothing beyond. My father had said, "A jackass is strong and he never went to school." Now my father was silent. I was working and earning money. That required no comment. The work was torment, he knew that. But this was a deep and personal problem which a man had to solve for himself—a problem my father had always had and had never solved. . . .

That year away from school had its value. I was out in the working world, mingling with all kinds of people of different nationalities and learning my way around. I lost a great deal of my shyness. I found out that although the Irish drank a little more, they were just as warmhearted and friendly as I considered the Italians. While the Jews liked business and trade, they would give you the shirt off their back if you needed it. While the Germans were sometimes overly self-assured and even pompous, it was to cover up their own feelings of inferiority or strangeness—just like the other immigrant groups.

Cranking the winch and attacking packing cases with my baling hook, traveling the elevated trains and eating in nickel joints, I found out that New York did not consist of merely Americans and Italians, but rather of people in varying stages of the thing called Americanization. While I could not have put these thoughts into words, I began to find myself reacting differently toward the bustling humanity around me.

When I returned to Morris High School, it was with a greater assurance and confidence. I no longer shied away from strangers, sticking to my own particular group, except when the day was over and I headed back to East Harlem. I no longer avoided the glance of a girl because her eyes were blue and her hair blond and her clothes expensive. . . .

I began to acquire a feeling for the English language and its sound and flavor. I knew many words I never dared use in conversation or in class, but which were there and fixed in my mind from reading and from constant use of the dictionary. I joined the literary club and wrote for the school paper. Then became an active member of the debating society.

During this period I was fascinated by the struggle of the Russian people to achieve some measure of freedom from the Czarist rule. For the debating society I wrote a speech defending the nihilists and their methods. "Why, you can't give this speech, Leonard," my teacher said. He was a quiet, soft-spoken man with a special knack for handling pupils. "You can't defend murder and bombing and bloodshed."

I grew hot under the collar. "The Czarist regime was all bloodshed," I argued. "Slavery and Lincoln and the Civil War. Mazzini and Garibaldi and the liberation of Italy. All bloodshed. Does justice begin where bloodshed leaves off, or does bloodshed begin where justice leaves off? Who knows, except there has never been any great movement for the liberation of a people without bloodshed."

I never made my high-school speech in defense of the nihilists. At the time I could not understand why I was not allowed to speak on the oppression of people. This, too, was an invaluable part of my education—that two wrongs don't make a right, that oppression can grow out of a revolt to overthrow oppression. But my intense interest has never wavered in the problems of social justice and minority groups, in the painful situations which we as immigrants had to face and which are faced today by Negroes and by those newcomers so often and disdainfully called "spicks" instead of Puerto Ricans.

At home I gave English lessons to Italian immigrants and charged from fifteen to twenty-five cents a session, depending upon the affluence of the student. Twenty-five cents for the man of private business and fifteen cents for the pushcart peddler and wage earner. "Maestro Professore," they would call me and bow respectfully to my mother and father, though neither of my parents ever had the patience to let me teach them more than a dozen English phrases. My mother would shoo me away with a tired gesture: "Don't bother me." My father would say, "In fifteen years I have not been able to make peace with that infernal language and you expect me to begin now? They call you 'Maestro Professore'? Good. I am happy. Happy for you and happy for myself. What little English I know is enough for the work for which I am paid."

With my father's pay, the money from my evening and weekend teaching, and what my brothers were earning, we were managing to get by. But my mother's health was no better. She had settled into a permanent kind of languor which slowly ate away the very life of her. . . .

Near the end of my last term at Morris High School I tried not to think about what the next year would bring. I closed my ears when my classmates mentioned the word "college." It was the promised land—college—but not for the likes of me. A friend, Harold Zoller, inadvertently made me face up to the idea. I'll never forget the day. At the high-school field day we had won a crazy three-legged race together. Arms locked about each other, my left leg strapped to his right, we hopped along leading all other contestants by several yards. We were both short—in fact, very similar in many ways, except that Zoller had blond wavy hair and a face made for easy laughter. We got along well together. He was the first of my close companions who did not live in East Harlem and who was not of Italian origin. He was the first non-Italian whose home I visited, a lovely brownstone house on 136th Street and Seventh Avenue. There I went through the gymnastics of trying to balance a teacup on my knee while his parents went out of their way to show their cordiality. In turn, I gathered up enough courage to ask him to our house for a spaghetti dinner. I also invited Mary, to weight the conversation a little more on the English side.

Zoller had a wonderful time in our dark, cramped rooms. It was his nature to enjoy himself no matter what the surroundings or circumstances. His frank, direct manner led him into any topic of conversation that came into his head. To him all people were alike, especially his friends, and he expected they would do pretty much what he was going to do himself. It was while Mary and I were walking him back across town to the streetcar that he stuck his hands, thumbs out, in his jacket pocket and, grinning to show how wonderful he felt with a mountain of spaghetti inside him, said, "Now what, Len? Have you made up your mind yet? Come to any decision?"

"What decision? What are you talking about?" Just the same I was sure of what was coming. I could feel it by the tightening of my collar and by a sudden desire to run away, though the subject had never been mentioned or discussed between us in any way.

"College, of course. What else did you think? Columbia is my choice." He laughed again. "I mean to say, my Dad's choice. But it's a great college, Len. You couldn't do better. Make up your mind, boy. How about Columbia?". . .

He swung up and into the trolley car and waved as it moved away down the avenue. I stood for a moment while Mary looked at me, her eyes questioning, waiting for the answer I hadn't been able to give Zoller.

"Don't you understand!" I said. "He's talking about college! Not high school. College costs money. Money I haven't got. Money I will never have. Money. Money. Money. I'm so sick of the sound of that word."

"People with less money and fewer qualifications than you have gone to college. It's all in how much you want to go."

"Let's not begin that all over again."

We walked along in silence. I was tired of hearing about what people with determination could do if they made up their minds. At this moment I didn't care. I was only concerned with the fact that my mother was sick and I had part of the responsibility of a family on my hands. I would go back to a full-time job and forget all about it.

"I suppose you've given up?" Mary said.

"There's nothing to give up. A simple fact. I can't go to college!"

"Have you ever heard of the Pulitzer Scholarship?"

I stopped and faced her. "What do you know about the Pulitzer Scholarship?"

"What everyone knows—that it is open to any high-school student who needs it and can pass the examinations. I also happen to know that your English teacher has already spoken to you about it. Miss Harding, that's her name. Isn't it so?"

"Have you any idea how many applicants there are for this scholarship from all over New York? Hundreds! I'd never make it.". . .

I had no belief in my going to college. I could see the long summer stretching ahead of me and the job I would have to find as a clerk or manual laborer. I thought about it all night and in the morning I still felt the same way. Think about a job, I said to myself. Nothing else.

During the English period I waited for the bell for us to change classes and then walked over to the desk where the teacher was seated. "Miss Harding," I said.

"Yes, Leonard."

"Is it too late—too late for the scholarship, I mean?"

Miss Harding rose from her desk. "I don't think so. We can call up the World Building from the principal's office and find out." She smiled and took hold of my arm. "Come on." As we went down the corridor she added, "I'm glad. I'm glad that you decided to take a chance."

❖   ❖   ❖

The American doctor was tall and gaunt and he stooped. With his pointed gray beard and black leather satchel he looked impressive. Miss Ruddy had sent him to us, and he had an excellent reputation. After spending an hour with my mother he came out, shrugging his shoulder. He glanced at my father, then at me, and moved slowly over to the window, looking down at the sidewalk four stories below. "I could guess. I wouldn't be sure. In a hospital we might be able to find out. Even then, I'm not sure."

"To an Italian, a hospital is just the same as a grave," I said.

He nodded. "She would never survive it. And here, her death is just as certain as if she were to jump out of this window. Anyway, keep her quiet. Rest as much as possible, and . . ." he cleared his throat, ". . . wait, that's all. Just wait."

When the doctor had gone I started to explain to my father, speaking in a whisper so that from the bedroom my mother could not overhear. It was hard to put into words the idea that for her it was all over. With a gesture my father motioned me to be quiet, as if to say that what the doctor had told us he had known for a long time. We sat together in silence. Then my father shook his head and let out a deep sigh. "For what?" he said. "For what? Leave home. Come to a strange land. All the suffering. To what purpose? For an end like this?"

This was in 1907—fifty-one years ago. My mother was dying. It was a sad summer for all of us at home. I had taken the college-entrance examinations for the Pulitzer Scholarship. It provided twenty-five dollars a month and free tuition in any school at Columbia, from engineering to medicine. I had taken the examinations but did not want to build my hopes around what seemed to me an impossible outside chance. . . .

❖ ❖ ❖

My mother died just before I entered Columbia. We buried her in the Calvary Cemetery in Brooklyn. . . .

In September, 1907, I began my studies at Columbia College with great expectations. I had been building in my mind what giant intellectual strides I would take in this famous institution of learning, how much knowledge I would acquire, how I would probe all resources and seek universal truths—the grandiose kind of ideas most boys have at this age, I suppose, except that my background and early training tended to make my dreams even more gigantic.

I was immediately jolted from my idealistic conception of a university by a battle between the freshmen and sophomores. The campus tradition was that a freshman's cap would be placed atop the flagpole. The sophomores would muster around the flagpole while our job as freshmen was to rush the pole and try to recover the cap. In this melee we punched and wrestled with each other until the upper classmen intervened, putting an end to the battle. We did not recover the cap and we were all pretty well roughed up on both sides. This was my introduction to Columbia. I remember limping from the campus with Garibaldi Lapolla, another East Harlem student who enrolled with me at the same time.

"Man alive!" Lapolla said, tucking in his torn shirt. "If the old folks could see us now! They'd think the whole bunch of us should be locked up in an asylum along with all the professors and the dean."

"Don't tell them," I advised. "Keep quiet." Experience had taught both of us that the spreading chasm which separated us from our parents could never again be bridged and that what happened to us in the outside world belonged to us alone. The challenge of newness and strangeness had to be met. . . .

Columbia was a disappointment to me in many ways. I concentrated on romance languages, with French as my major. Natural inclination urged me to Italian, but these were still the days when it was fashionable to forget Italian. To have prepared myself to teach Italian would have seriously limited my possibilities of earning a living. Already the idea of teaching in some form or another had begun to formulate in my mind.

We rushed around the campus from one class to another. Science. Mathematics. Philosophy. Chemistry. Spanish. French. History. And a class in Dante in which I was the only student. There were many courses but with no unifying principle about which we could center our attention. The courses were, for the most part, easy—too easy. The demands upon us were high-schoolish for the most part, not mature. There were lectures and quizzes, but not enough real teaching and little rapport between student and instructor. In short, the idea of the dedicated life of the student which I had learned as a boy in Avigliano was not met by what I was receiving here.

I tried to explain it to Mary. "There is no contact of minds. You feel that the professor is niggardly about the knowledge he hands out—as if he were afraid he might give too much at one time. You go to a lecture and listen and simply accept. What kind of education do you call this?"

She hesitated a moment. "It's education to prepare you to live in a competitive society, I suppose."

"But you can be a dope and still be a gentleman," I said. "That is, if you make one of the varsity teams. You learn history. You reach back into the civilizations of the past. What for? Where is the relationship with the present, with the problems of the world today, with the life here in East Harlem, with the things which concern you and me?"

"You've just got to make the connection yourself," Mary said. "The student who can't surmount these difficulties is not cut out to be a scholar."

I smiled. "The trouble with you is you never attack—you're always defending everything."

I was the student, she knew, who wanted to be the scholar. Within me too was the desire to be accepted and to form a part of the world in which I found myself. In spite of my Italian origin and the place where I lived, I felt I deserved to belong.

So when the captain asked me to try out for the varsity soccer team because of my record at Morris High, I consented, in spite of my feeling that it was much more important for a student to devote himself to his studies.

That afternoon as we were going down the long steps leading from Morningside Drive in the direction of East Harlem, Garibaldi Lapolla said intensely, "You've got to make the soccer team, Len. Show them that we've got the stuff."

We were joined by John La Guardia, who used to walk with us. "What stuff? What are you fellows talking about?" he exclaimed, catching the drift. "Why should we have to prove anything? I'm sick and tired of making excuses for myself. Here I've been calling myself John B. La Guardia. What's this *John* La Guardia? Who am I fooling? John is not the name my father gave me. Beginning tomorrow, it's going to be Giovanni Battista La Guardia. On every examination paper and everything I sign, and the hell with what anybody thinks!"...

The reaction was setting in. What at one time we were ashamed of, must now be brought into the open. How else could we make peace with our souls? Had it been in my power, I am sure I would have returned the "i" which Mrs. Cutter of the Soup School had dropped from Coviello. But names have strength and a character of their own and are not played with easily. Covello persisted, inasmuch as the dropping of an "i" no way altered its Italian origin. . . .

❖ ❖ ❖

After considerable difficulty and petitioning, a group of us from the Home Garden, led by Michael Scilipoti, convinced the board of directors of the Young Men's Christian Association of the need for a YMCA branch in East Harlem. Four thousand dollars was made available to us with the stipulation that we match this figure with a thousand dollars in neighborhood pledges of our own. We worked night and day, going from house to house and from store to store, speaking to merchants and business and professional men, trying to raise the money; generally we faced the argument, "If the young people want a club, let them pay for it themselves."

We managed to get the money after great difficulty, some of it in cash, most of it in pledges. Actually, we were able to raise only eight hundred dollars, but the project went through just the same. We rented a brownstone building at 322 East 116th Street and the work of reconditioning began. Gradually, as a result of our day-and-night labor, the back yard began to look like a handball and basketball court, as well as a place for gymnastic drills. The kitchen was transformed into a dressing and shower room. The dining room on the ground floor was converted into a poolroom, on the theory that if young men had to play pool it was better for them to play it in wholesome surroundings. On the main floor there was the secretary's office, which was also used for small conferences, and there was a large conference and recreation room.

In September of 1910 we officially and proudly opened the doors
of the East Harlem YMCA. Membership was three dollars a year with
nominal fees for educational classes, gymnasium, and other special
activities. We had a dramatic club, a music club, and a literary society.
On Sunday afternoons there were lectures and concerts and intellectual discussions. We got the traveling branch of the New York Public
Library to lend us hundreds of books in all fields, but particularly
books on Italy. By now we had come to the full realization of how important it was to learn about our Italian culture and our place in
American life. First of all we needed to know as much as possible
about ourselves before we could feel that our people and their culture
were not inferior—only different.

It was in connection with my work at the East Harlem YMCA that
I came in contact with two men who were to have a decided influence
in my life—an Italian immigrant by the name of Leone Piatelli, and an
American-born New Englander named John A. Shedd. Piatelli was a
poet who earned his living as a bookkeeper; Shedd, secretary to an
American millionaire, had fallen in love with Italy and was doing vol-
unteer religious work among the Italians of New York City.

Lost and wandering in the intellectual void of East Harlem, Piatelli
was instinctively drawn to those of us who were going to college and
could converse in Italian. It was after one of my English classes he was
attending that he waited for me in the reception room and we walked
down the street together. His manner was vibrant, alive. "We must
teach Dante!" he exclaimed. "We must. There is an historical parallel
between the development of Italy and the development of America. In
his *Divina Commedia*, Dante lit the torch of civil liberty and national
consciousness in Italy. The universality of his dream asserted itself in
Italy through such men as Giuseppe Mazzini—and in America
through Abraham Lincoln. The two seem to have been fashioned by
the same hand."

I left Piatelli, my mind tingling. I could not sleep. I knocked on the
door of the Accurso flat, where I knew Mary would still be awake,
reading or correcting the papers of her students at the grammar school.
Together we went up to the roof of the tenement where the night was a
deep blue-black with pinpricks of stars. Below and around us were the
lights of the city, and over on the river the tugs and barges and smaller
moving craft.

"You must meet this Piatelli. You'll like him. With mind and instinct he touches the truth. Dante, Mazzini, Lincoln! I never thought
about them together before. Why? And now a casual meeting with a

man who is almost a perfect stranger has given me a new feeling of direction. How I like this man!"

"I'm glad," Mary said. "You need friends like him—men who will excite you."

It was true. Leone Piatelli fired me with the desire to know more about the world of poetry and art and literature and to bring it all into relation to my own life. *"Il mistero della vita,"* as he phrased it in Italian. "The riddle of existence."

Mary and I stood together, silent for a time, looking over the rooftops of East Harlem. Both of us wondered, I am sure, how out of these tenements and the turbulence of human existence could emerge beauty of mind and spirit.

It is a strange coincidence that John Shedd, whom I met just a short time later at the YMCA, was an ardent admirer of Abraham Lincoln and over a period of years had acquired an extensive personal library dealing with Lincolniana. Shedd was the exact opposite of Piatelli. He was nearly twice Piatelli's age, close to fifty, heavily built, and in appearance much like G. K. Chesterton, with a massive head, flowing gray hair, straggly mustache, and bushy eyebrows curling out over the edges of the thick lenses of his pince-nez. His laughter was a hearty bellow that shook his whole frame. He loved people and living and had to be in the center of things.

John Shedd and his wife had been teaching Sunday School in a little Italian Protestant mission on Cherry Street downtown. They helped out financially by their own donations and by soliciting funds from the St. Paul's Methodist Church at 86th Street and West End Avenue, just a few blocks from their home. His interest in Italy and Italians brought him to our branch of the YMCA.

Like a big, overgrown sheep dog he began poking around, wanting to know all about our program and activities. Almost before anyone realized it, he was on the board of directors and closely identified with every aspect of our work among the Italians. He loved pithy sayings, used them often in conversation—in fact wrote a little book of aphorisms called "Salt from My Attic."

"Leonard," he would suddenly say, "when we act the clown, we ought to be sure that we have a clown's audience"; or "Your man with downcast eyes forever sees dirt. There are no stars in the heavens for him"; and "Tell me what you love, and I will tell you what you are."

"I have never been in Florence," he told me at one of our first meetings, "but I know it as if I had been born there. The *Arno*. The *Ponte Vecchio. Gl' Uffizi. Piazza della Signoria.* Michelangelo's David. The beautiful bronze doors of Ghiberti that Michelangelo said could be the doors of Paradise. I can close my eyes and see it all. I can smell the odor of chestnuts and bread baking in the ovens. All—all there in the back of my mind like the little New England town where I was born.". . .

❖   ❖   ❖

While working for my master's degree, openings to teach French occurred at Wesleyan and Syracuse Universities. Here was an opportunity to realize my goal—a professorship. Yet the pay was such that I could not possibly afford to take either of these jobs. To do so would have meant leaving New York, where I could augment a modest salary with outside work. Besides, I still wanted to contribute financially to my family. Instead, I took the examinations of the Board of Education and qualified as a teacher of French in the New York City public schools.

❖   ❖   ❖

A classmate of mine at Columbia, Angelo Lipari, was teaching French as a substitute at De Witt Clinton High School and the job seemed too much for him. Ordinarily of even temper, the last few months had made him very nervous. One night when we were sitting around at the YMCA, he blurted, "Confound those brats. As much as I like to teach, I can't stand them any longer."

"What? What's the matter? " I said.

"What's the matter? You never had to teach roughnecks like this. A different bunch every hour. Six hours a day. Monsters, planning and scheming how they can torment and tantalize you!"

I laughed and scratched my head. "You're making a mountain out of a molehill. You can handle them."

"You don't get it," Lipari insisted. "You don't understand what it is because you haven't been through it yourself. *No one can teach them.*"

It was only a few weeks later that Lipari came to me bubbling with excitement. An opportunity had come at last for him to teach at one of the New England colleges. He wanted me to take over his classes at De Witt Clinton. He had even arranged an interview for me with the principal, Dr. Tildsley. This was in December, a month before the end of the fall term. I was at Columbia working for my master's degree. Here was an opportunity I could not afford to turn down.

The next day I met Dr. John L. Tildsley, who for the next quarter of a century—first as principal of De Witt Clinton and later as Assistant

Superintendent of the High School Division—was to exert a great influence on my academic career in the New York City schools. Stocky, square of jaw, as determined as he looked, Dr. Tildsley, after examining my credentials, asked me only one question. "Where did you go to high school?"

"Morris High."

"Then you know what a high-school job is like. Go upstairs to the lunchroom. Your class is waiting there."

Upstairs I found some forty teen-age boys sprawling around on tables and benches, yawning, bored, waiting for amusement. Obviously, because of the shortage of classroom space, the lunchroom was also to be my classroom for the time being. While the students sized me up, I selected a table and made it my desk. Before they could come to any conclusion, I folded my arms and, staring straight at them said, "My name is Leonard Covello. I'm your new French teacher. Now get out your books and let's get to work.". . .

❖   ❖   ❖

Our YMCA branch, now in the third year of its operation, was finding it increasingly difficult to fulfill the yearly pledge of a thousand dollars to the central board. Despite the excellent work we were doing, the active interest of the young men of East Harlem, our increasing membership, and, above all, the great need for such work, it looked as if we might have to close our door. The fact that all of our services were voluntary and no salary was paid except to the secretary, Lawson Brown, who received the niggardly sum of seventy-five dollars a month and gave practically twenty-four hours a day to his work, did not make any difference. We still had to meet a pledge of a thousand dollars. As usual, the merchants and people of means would not come to our rescue. It was the same old story. If the young men of East Harlem wanted a recreation and educational center, they could pay for it themselves.

Also it became apparent that the state YMCA board was concerned with large projects which handled young men by the thousands and whose buildings would be landmarks in a community. In vain we pleaded that the work of our little center be continued, citing the case of Miss Ruddy and the Home Garden and the contribution she had made to a whole neighborhood with what in the beginning had been a one-room mission. We felt that a more effective job could be done in small units where greater attention could be given the individual. But we lost our case. The YMCA of East Harlem was closed.

❖   ❖   ❖

It was an odd thing that while Italian was not taught in any of the city high schools, it was still possible to get credit for it if a student could pass the New York State examinations, known as the Regents' Examinations.

One day while I was on lunchroom duty, three students approached me. Two of them were former pupils from one of my French classes—Hannibal De Bellis, who later became a physician, and Steve Calarco, who first went into law and is now in the wholesale fruit business. The third I knew only by sight and because of his reputation as an athlete and his participation in various school activities. His name was Benny Segreto. Only about five feet six inches tall, he had rugged shoulders and powerful arms. His face was full, and an exceptional strength and determination showed in it in the rare moments while he wasn't smiling and joking. I had heard him speak with considerable force at meetings of the student council, and his accent tagged him as coming from the island of Sicily.

He stood there now, his hands in his pockets, listening politely while De Bellis and Calarco explained that they wanted to take the Regents' Examinations in Italian and needed extra coaching.

"Hannibal and I were both born in Italy," Steve explained.

"What we're trying to find out is if we know enough to pass this examination. You're the boss."

We all laughed. Benny Segreto now spoke for the first time. "They know very much, Mr. Covello. I speak with them. I have studied Italian in Palermo."

The tenor of his voice had nothing of boastfulness. Here was a simple statement of fact. Immediately I was curious to the ultimate purpose of his schooling. Despite his genial smile and warmth of manner, there was a boundary beyond which intimacy was not invited. In his glance one could almost sense the pride of people who have both Mediterranean and Arab blood in their veins.

❖   ❖   ❖

In September, 1920, [after returning from the war and ten months of employment in advertising,] I again stepped into a classroom and looked into the faces of about twenty-five boys who formed my first class in Italian at De Witt Clinton, perhaps the only Italian class in any public school in the country at that time. Our efforts and struggles prior to the war had succeeded, and there was a deep satisfaction in this achievement. Surely the language and culture of Italy held a place beside that of France, Germany, or Spain. Surely the student from the lower or upper East Side had a right to that spiritual lift that comes from knowing that the achievements of one's people have been recognized.

For this basic belief those of us who espoused this simple cause [of getting Italian language taught] were often criticized by fellow teachers and by the general public. They argued that we were keeping the boys "foreigners." The boys were in America now and should use English exclusively. I was myself accused of "segregating" my students, and more than once by Italian-Americans themselves. The war had strengthened the idea of conformity. Americanization meant the casting off of everything that was "alien," especially the language and culture of national origin. Yet the amazing paradox lay in the fact that it was perfectly all right for the Italo-American boy to study Latin or French, German or Spanish.

Fortunately, at De Witt Clinton, we had the approval of Dr. Francis H. Paul, the principal, who was sympathetic with our point of view. It was he who had made the *Circolo* [an Italian study organization] possible in the first place and who had later approved the introduction of the teaching of Italian.

Dr. Paul called me into his office one day not long after my return and spoke about the problem of the rapidly increasing number of students of Italian origin now coming to Clinton from all over the city. "These boys are not easy to handle," he said, sitting on the edge of his desk. "To put it bluntly, it will be your job to look after these boys. I will see to it that your schedule is changed so that you will have time to take care of them. In short, Leonard, from now on I want you to be the father-confessor of these East Side boys."

In an out-of-the-way corner of the old De Witt Clinton building, I found a small room that was being used as a stock room. Together with some of my students I spent several Saturdays cleaning and painting and putting it in shape for an office. The room had a very narrow window and just enough space for a desk, a few file cabinets, some chairs, and a mimeographing machine. It wasn't much of an office, but it was good enough for a beginning. It was good enough for the first office of the first Italian Department in the public schools of New York City.

In this two-by-four office I held conferences, handled disciplinary problems, interviewed parents, and planned our work. For the very first time in my experience as a teacher I began to have a feeling of inner satisfaction which rose from the knowledge that here was a job that I really wanted to do. All my thoughts about a professorship or becoming a medical doctor faded, never to be revived. No longer was I merely teaching a language or a subject. Here I was grappling with *all* the problems affecting the boys coming to me for help.

Often I would be working in my office, late in the afternoon, and a knock would come on the door, hesitant, reluctant, and I would know at once that it was another of my boys coming to me for help or advice. When the knock came during school hours I could almost be sure it had to do with a school problem. But when it sounded out of the stillness of the deserted corridors, I could be equally sure that the problem was a personal one.

At this moment I can still see Joe D'Angelo sitting in the chair near my desk. He was a tall boy, weighing about one hundred and eighty pounds, dressed in a new suit and carrying a derby. To make it easier for him to talk I kept my eyes on the narrow knot of his tie while he fumbled to explain why he had come. He was going to a party. His companions were waiting for him outside the school. "I had to see you first, Mr. Covello. I gotta get this thing off my chest. It's the old man. He keeps hittin' me all the time. No matter what I say or do he's gotta start cloutin' me. He's a big guy and he works on the docks, and it hurts, and I can't stand it no more."

"If he really hurts you. . . " I started to say.

Joe D'Angelo shook his head. "That's not it." He held out a bony fist across the desk for my observation. "What he don't know is I've been fighting around the Jersey clubs a lot under the name of Kid Angel. I'm pretty good. That's what he don't know. If I hit him I could put him in the hospital. That's what I'm scared of. It's gonna happen and it would kill my mother."

After a silence I said, "How is it you never told them at home about the boxing?"

"Because ever since I was a little kid my mother has been telling everybody that I was going to be a lawyer."

"While you want to be a fighter?"

"No. I want to be a lawyer. But I make a couple of bucks in these club matches. I get a kick out of it, and I don't have to work in a store or a factory after school. Only thing is, I could never make them believe it."

I sent Joe off to his party and told him to spend the night with his uncle who lived in the Bronx. Then I took the subway downtown to the "Little Italy" of Greenwich Village. The D'Angelo family lived in one of those red brick tenements on MacDougal Street. As I entered the downstairs hall and caught the odor of garlic and tomato sauce, I felt right at home. Pappa D'Angelo himself, clad in his undershirt, answered the door. He was short, with heavy shoulders and a gray mustache, and an iron-gray stubble of hair covered his head and became a mattress of gray on his chest. He looked at me, wiped his mouth with a bright, checkered napkin, and was about to slam the door in my face. When he caught the name De Witt Clinton, his manner changed.

"*Perdona!* Scuse me, please. I think you was selling piano or something." He gently took hold of my arm and ushered me inside, directly into the kitchen. "Ninitta," he said to the middle-aged woman seated at the table. "Get up. Get one more plate. Is the teacher from the school where Joe go. Clintona." Suddenly he stopped dead. "Is Joe?" he shouted. "What he do? He do something bad? That why you here? I kill him! I break all the bones in his head!"

The mother started to cover her face with her hands in anticipation of some terrible calamity. I took hold of the father's arm and, wagging my free hand in a characteristic Italian gesture, at the same time speaking in the Neapolitan dialect, said, "Who said anything about Joe being a bad boy? Joe is a good boy. He is a very good student."

When both father and mother got over the staggering fact that I could not only speak Italian but could even speak their dialect, they made me sit down and eat a dish of sausage and peppers. "It is an honor. You will do us a great honor, Signor Maestro," Pappa D'Angelo insisted, in the most flowery language at his command. "Also a glass of wine. A gentle glass of wine made with my own hands. So he is a good student, Giuseppe? And good he should be." He extended a massive paw. "With this instrument I have taught him right from wrong. Respect for his elders. For those who instruct him in school. In the old tradition. In this way he will become educated and become a lawyer and not work on the docks like his father."

"Exactly," I agreed, rolling a mouthful of wine over my tongue. "It is just this that I have come to see you about. Giuseppe is getting too big. You have to handle him differently, now."

"I have been telling him this again and again," the mother broke in.

"Quiet," Pappa D'Angelo said. "Where is the harm in a father correcting his son? This is something new. Something American. I have heard of it but I do not understand. Only this very evening I had to give Giuseppe a lesson in economy. A derby! Imagine, a boy buying and wearing a derby. To go to work in a factory!"

"With me," I said, "it was shiny shoes with buttons. Besides it was his own money—money that he earned with his own hands."

"Which changes nothing at all."

"But which makes for impatience and loss of temper. He is getting too old for you to knock him around. He is afraid that one day he is going to forget himself and hurt you. That is what he is afraid of."

It was a joke. Pappa D'Angelo started to laugh. He downed a full glass of wine and heaved his powerful chest. "Ha, ha. Now he thinks he can lick his pappa." He slammed his fist down on the table. "Wait he come home, I show him. I show him who the boss in this house, lilla snotnose! " All of a sudden he was so mad at his son again that he could only talk the language of the docks.

"Wait a minute," I said. "Calm down. Do you know what kind of work your son does when he is not in school? Do you know how he makes the money that he gives you here at home and that paid for the derby?"

I told them then as simply as I could that their son was not work-ing in a factory but was making money as a prize fighter.

The father did not get it right away. "A fighter," he asked, "with the hands?"

"With the hands. A boxer. I have been told that even though he is very young, he is good. He would have a future as a fighter. But Joe does not want to be a fighter. He fights so that he can earn money to be a lawyer. But he is afraid when you beat him that someday he is going to forget you are his father."

"*Madonna!*" the mother breathed.

Pappa D'Angelo rocked his head. After a while, as if this were not enough, he scratched it furiously. He looked at me sheepishly. He started to smile. The smile broadened into a grin.

"That lilla sonamangonia!" he said.

That was my encounter with the D'Angelo family. There were so many others in those days that sometimes it seems as if I spent al-most as much time in the homes of my students as I did at the school. There was Nick Barone, who didn't show up in class for a couple of days. He worked on an ice wagon after school, and one of the big ice blocks toppled over and smashed his hand, landing him in the hospital. Nick had spoken to me about his parents. They could speak no English at all and both mother and father worked at home doing stitching and needle piece work for the garment industry—the common exploitation of the time. They had little or no contact at all with the outside world.

The Barone family lived in the Italian section around 28th Street and Second Avenue. I went there after school and found the small tenement flat in a state of turmoil—crowded with neighbors, and the mother and father carrying on so that I thought for sure that Nick had passed away. When I was finally able to make them understand who I was, both parents grabbed my hands, imploring me to save Nick before it was too late.

"He will die there," the father lamented. "Everyone knows what goes on in a hospital—the last stage before the grave. A soul could die in a torment of thirst and no one would lift a finger to bring you a glass of water."

"Old superstitions about hospitals," I sought to explain; "stories from the old country when distances were great and knowledge of medicine limited and the patient almost always died before reaching the hospital. It is different now."

"But we could take such wonderful care of him at home here," the mother entreated. "I could cook him a chicken, make him broth and pastina and food to get well. The good Lord knows what they will feed him there, if anything."

After I had managed to calm them somewhat, I had both the mother and father put on their best clothes and I took them to the hospital, where up until now they had not dared to go. We found Nick sitting up in bed, joking with a nurse and having a gay time with his companions in the ward. When one of the internes even spoke to them in Italian, their attitude changed to one of great wonderment.

On the way home from the hospital the father turned to me with an expression of guilt and deep embarrassment. "You must forgive us. There are many things here we know nothing about. It is hard to change old ideas and the way we think even though we see the changes every day in our children." He shook his head. "If only everybody in the world could speak the same tongue, then perhaps things would not be quite so hard to understand." And the more I came into contact with the family life of my boys, the more I became aware of the vital importance of language in the double orientation—to family and to community —of the immigrant child. . . .

❖   ❖   ❖

One of the chief problems in the early years of the Italian Department was the lack of adequate texts with which to teach the language. We found that existing Italian textbooks were too advanced for those of our students who had had no previous foreign-language instruction. And their limited knowledge of the Italian dialect heard at home was of little value to them.

Working with one of my assistants, Annita Giacobbe, I prepared a beginner's textbook. We started it in 1923. In 1927 it was published by The Macmillan Company under the title of *First Book in Italian*. It took us four years to get this book into its final shape, and it covered only the first two years of the Italian course. We spent a tremendous amount of time on each lesson to perfect it. Annita Giacobbe and I would outline a plan in my little office. Some of the older boys from the Italian Department would type the stencils and run the mimeograph machine which turned out the materials to be tried out in class. Then the lesson would be revised, the students giving their views, and the mimeograph machine started all over again. Without the help of the boys themselves, Annita Giacobbe and I could never have found the time or energy to complete this text which, we were determined, would attract and not repel the student. After many conferences, the publisher finally agreed to allow us illustrations for the book, which greatly enhanced its appeal and educational value.

If I had put the same amount of time and energy into the preparation of a French or Spanish text, I would have made a great deal more money. But I am sure that Annita Giacobbe, seated today in her little villa in Sicily, will agree with me that the satisfaction we derived in creating an Italian book for our boys was by far the greater part of the compensation we received for our effort. . . .

❖   ❖   ❖

Something occurred which marked the beginning of a new era in my career as a teacher. I was invited to teach a Spanish course at New York University. While I was teaching there I persuaded the Dean of the School of Commerce to allow me to start an elementary class in Italian. Before long the number of students increased to a point where I asked my assistant at De Witt Clinton, Annita Giacobbe, to take over some of the classes.

The room in which I taught at New York University was also used by Professor Paul Radosavljevich, a Yugoslav, who taught Experimental Education. Professor Rado, everyone called him. Often I would arrive early and sit in on his course while waiting for my own class to begin. Slowly I became engrossed, fascinated by this hulking, articulate European who had been so thoroughly and carefully trained as a scholar and could express himself with equal facility in English, German, and the Slavic languages. Often after our work we would stop at some little Italian restaurant in Greenwich Village and have a bite to eat and a glass of wine together. "Study for your doctorate, Leonard," Professor Rado advised after he began to understand something of my interest in immigrant problems. "In order to help your people you must advance in the educational system. Become at least a superintendent of schools. Concentrate on the ethnic factor in education. That is your field—the cultural factor in education—a subject a great many educators talk about, but very few actually understand."

Under the influence of Professor Rado I felt a new incentive to continue my education and began to take educational courses for my doctorate. Out of our talks the idea grew in my mind of doing a comprehensive study on the social background of the Southern Italian. In order to cope with problems dealing with the education of the immigrant and his American child, it was first necessary to have all the information I could accumulate. "For instance," I explained to Professor Rado, "in the mind of the average Southern Italian immigrant a constant tug-of-war takes place. I run up against it all the time. On the one hand he wants his son to have the advantages of an education never possible for himself, and on the other, centuries of tradition tell him that a boy must work, have responsibility, and contribute to the family. These are not easy to reconcile—school and work. In the average family it leads to a great deal of friction."

In order to know more about our boys we devised a questionnaire for them to fill out. We wanted the usual information such as age, home address, subjects the student was taking, teacher's name beside each subject, recreational interests, but also other data—if he worked after school, success in passing subjects, cause of failure, details of home environment, and particularly in what way we could help him. Through this questionnaire and by means of personal interviews, we were beginning to find out what was happening in school and out of school and also getting glimpses of life in the Italian communities. "We want to know more—we have to know more about this thing everyone keeps referring to as the Americanization process.". . .

"Tell me, Paul," I added, "where is the source of cultural strength for the immigrant—any immigrant?"

"That is easy. The source of cultural strength for any immigrant must be the country of his birth. Until the immigrant can be assimilated to a point where he begins to draw from American sources, he must look backward into the past. That is why, Leonard, you must write your doctor's thesis on the cultural or ethnic factor in education."

❖   ❖   ❖

On the lower East Side of New York City, around 10th Street, there was a large building known as the Boys' Club of New York. In 1927 its Board of Directors and other interested citizens created another branch and purposely located it in East Harlem, where there was a high incidence of juvenile delinquency. Several years later, a grant of thirty-six thousand dollars was made available to the School of Education of New York University for a study of the effect of a boys' club program upon a local community and its problems. This East Harlem branch at 111th Street near First Avenue, with its six thousand members, was elected as the laboratory for the study. The research project was headed by a Chicago sociologist, Frederic M. Thrasher, whose book *The Gang: A Study of 1313 Gangs in Chicago* had become a classic in its field.

Before the study, many striking claims had been made favoring the establishment of clubs for adolescents. Judge Arnold of Chicago stated that the Union League Boys' Club in that city caused a decline of 73 per cent in juvenile crime in the district it served, and that in the neighborhood of the downtown Boys' Club of New York 60 per cent less juvenile delinquency is found than in other similar areas on the lower East Side. It was to test the validity of this assumption that the study in East Harlem was undertaken. In order to secure complete impartiality, the Boys' Club of New York took the initiative in having a university, through its department of sociology, undertake the research project.

I received a note from Dr. Thrasher and went to see him at his office at the University at Washington Square. He was a rather slender man, casual in his manner, though his eyes betrayed a constant interest in life around him. He shook hands and motioned me to an armchair while he closed the door of his office, then leaned back against the desk, facing me. "Have you heard about our little project?" he asked.

"Some. I'm deeply interested."

"I thought you would be. This club is in the neighborhood where you grew up. Many of the boys are Clinton students. This will be the first research project to attempt a community case study of this type. We will try to evaluate scientifically the work of such a club and try to estimate its importance in curbing delinquency. Furthermore, we want to understand the educative processes that go on in such a community."

This project fascinated me. It fitted in very well with my idea for a doctoral thesis on the social background of the Southern Italian immigrant. We would be studying every aspect of the life of the community of East Harlem which at that time consisted of ninety thousand Italian-Americans—the largest community of its kind in the United States.

When the Boys' Club study got under way, De Witt Clinton High School was still located at 59th Street near Tenth Avenue. Since a large number of our students came from East Harlem, it was possible to get a great deal of our information right in the classroom by means of questionnaires, personal interviews, and individual case studies. Much of this material related to family, background, leisure activities, and future plans, especially concerning their life work. These were highly personal questions that had to be asked with warmth and sympathy.

In this study I was aided, as always, by Annita Giacobbe. Her natural understanding of the boys led them to an unburdening of confidences that would have been extremely difficult with any other teacher. I was also helped a great deal by my older students and a former Clinton boy, Salvatore Cimilluca, who had graduated from Cornell and was working for his master's degree as a participant in the Boys' Club study. Sal could speak the Italian dialects as well as the English of the streets. His easy, friendly manner gained him entrance into any home. "Signora," he would say, bunching his fingers together, "you're talking to me, Salvatore Cimilluca. My father came over on the same boat with you. Now then, what is the real reason that the truant officer keeps coming after your son, Mario? "

"The real reason, *figlio mio*, is that we need him in the vegetable store. And on top of that the real, real reason is that little Mario has a better head for turnips than he has for study. That even God himself would not deny."

The techniques, the methods of investigation, and the information when compiled and analyzed formed the basis of new sociological thought and focus on the problems of minority groups in high-delinquency areas. And the Boys' Club study did a great deal for me personally. My association with Dr. Thrasher and the other sociologists opened a completely new vista in the field of education for me. I was now convinced that to achieve educational objectives, it was necessary to have complete and detailed knowledge of every aspect of the lives of the people to be educated.

A few hours each week I had been going to The Hamilton House, a settlement house on the lower East Side, and talking informally to a group of social workers. They asked questions about things they did not understand concerning Italian immigrant families and I answered these questions to the best of my knowledge, drawing upon my own personal experience, the contacts with my students, what I had read, and the conclusions I had drawn from my study of the subject. "Why is it," one of these workers asked me one night, "that the Italian mother plays so unimportant a role in the household?"

"It merely appears so. Tradition has had it for countless generations that the woman shall be inconspicuous. On the surface it still seems so, but be assured that hardly any major decision takes place in an Italian home without the mother having a major part in that decision."

These sessions were stimulating for me because they made me think, made me remember aspects of Italian life I had forgotten, helped me in my sociological studies and with the material I was beginning to gather for my dissertation. By this time I had come to the belief that a regular course concerning the Italian immigrant should be given at the University. . . .

As I look back to that period of my life now known for some reason obscure to me as the roaring twenties, I am impressed by how small beginnings developed, expanded, and gathered momentum. For instance, a casual talk with a student who was having difficulty maintaining himself in school because his father had died led to the creation of a Student Welfare Committee, and in turn, student scholarship aid. I relied upon the reaction of my boys to the problems they were facing to develop ways and means at Clinton to grapple with these problems.

Listening to the stories of the boys who were failures in the eyes of the school, and particularly in their own eyes, we tried to work out special programs for them. With a very devoted group of teachers, many of whom were not Italian, such as Dr. John McCarthy, Miss Catherine Griffin, Dr. Abraham Kroll, and Bertha Mandel, we used to meet during lunchtime and at times after school hours and discuss the problems of individual failure and what could be done. In his position as administrative assistant of the school, Abe Kroll helped many a difficult boy who found himself in a tight situation or was on the verge of expulsion from school. . . .

It became increasingly apparent that there was a pressing need for initiating and promoting educational programs within these "ethnic islands." There were hundreds of Italo-American societies in these communities—fraternal, mutual aid, sporting, professional, religious, and purely social. In characteristic fashion, each club or society worked within its own small circle. While they were aware and concerned about the problems that all Italians faced, they were ineffective because they had not learned to unite and to work as a group on a city-wide basis. This was one of the important purposes of the Casa Italiana Educational Bureau.

We compiled the names of all the Italo-American organizations in the metropolitan area and invited delegates from these societies to attend a monthly meeting at the Casa Italiana to discuss educational and social problems affecting Italo-Americans everywhere. We also created a speakers' bureau, with outstanding people in the educational field, to travel around and give lectures at various centers.

We were able to gather and publish valuable material on such topics as "Occupational Trends among Italians in New York City," "The Padrone or 'Boss' System" (exploitation of immigrants by their own kind), "Some Contributions of Italy and Her Sons to American Life," "The Italian Population of New York City," and the cataloguing of information which had never before been attempted with specific reference to the Italians as an ethnic group in America. This information was of great use to those of us seeking to penetrate the maze of rumors and contradictory notions concerning a particular people. It was as if we were fumbling in the dark until suddenly a crack of light entered and we began to see and understand and evaluate ideas and theories in terms of statistics and hard facts.

Because of my association with the Casa Italiana activities, I was asked to become a member of the Folk Festival Council of New York City, sponsored by the Foreign Language Information Service, which had been started during the First World War to work with immigrant groups. My job was to organize an Italian group to participate with other nationality groups in fostering native folk songs and dances. I remember the enthusiasm which greeted this project when I broached the idea to a number of my pupil-teachers at New York University and my associates at the Casa Italiana.

"What do you think?" I asked. "Are we capable of putting such a project across? Can we compete with the other groups? "

Elba Farabegoli, one of the group, looked at me in amazement. "What do you mean, can we compete? I know a great deal about folk music. And I believe we could even get Maestro Benelli, who toured the United States with the Florentine Choir, to be our director."

Miss Farabegoli put a great deal of time and energy into the formation of the Italian Choral Society, which is still functioning today as the Coro D'Italia. Through her efforts, we were able to secure the services of Maestro Benelli, whose musical knowledge and extraordinary ability enabled us to include in our repertoire a fine collection of folk songs that had their origins anywhere from Trieste to Sicily. We acquired authentic Italian costumes, and the interest of people who could instruct in the folk dances knew no bounds. Before long we were performing with other units of the Folk Festival Council at the International House, Town Hall, The Guild Theatre, Channon Theatre, and the mall in Central Park.

Here was another contribution of immigrant peoples to the cultural life of America. All these activities were a far cry from my initial plans. Where was the serious university professor who would dedicate his life to the romance languages? Where the calm, cloistered life of the college campus? My old friend, Leone Piatelli, grown leaner and sadder than ever from his struggles with the depression, said to me, "Leonardo, you go rushing around as if you had been bitten by a tarantula. When do you ever find time to sleep?". . .

❖   ❖   ❖

For twenty-two years I was principal of Benjamin Franklin High School. During that time we moved from old buildings, originally annexes of De Witt Clinton, one of which dated as far back as the Civil War, to a large and beautiful red brick Georgian structure on the East River Drive.

For twenty-two years I served a school devoted to the education of boys who, in the estimation of the outside world, offered one of the greatest crime potentials of any section in the country. For twenty-two years I served a part of New York City which was looked upon by many people as a pariah community.

Now that I have retired, I look back upon these years as the most fruitful period of my life. I believe that to serve one's community and to be involved in the education of growing boys is the most rewarding task a human being can undertake.

One of the biggest problems in connection with the establishment of Benjamin Franklin was the staff. It was necessary to get good teachers, dedicated teachers, teachers who not only had the necessary scholastic background but who also understood growing boys. We had to have strong men and women, with feeling for and understanding of particular types of boys—boys from immigrant communities, whose parents often had very recently arrived. East Harlem spread itself over an area of one hundred sixty square blocks and had a population of over 200,000 souls—a city the size of Syracuse and yet lost and unknown except for those of us who lived there. Negro rubbed shoulders with white. Italians, Puerto Ricans, Jews, Germans, Irish lived down the street from each other. One of the first surveys made of the student body of Benjamin Franklin High showed that it included thirty-four different nationalities.

Quite a few teachers transferred from De Witt Clinton, among them Dr. Morris Deshel, Dina Di Pino, Annita Giacobbe, and Dr. Abraham Kroll, who came as my administrative assistant. A dryly humorous, pipe-smoking New Englander by the name of Austin Works, who was chairman of English in a New York City high school, also joined our staff. He exerted a great influence on our boys, who affectionately dubbed him "Mr. Woiks."

We had hardly settled in the old building on East 108th Street when Austin Works came to my office on the second floor to tell me how pleased he was he had made the decision to transfer to Franklin. . . .

Most of our ablest teachers were those who came to Franklin of their own volition. Among them was our Dean of Boys, Sal Pergola. Born in New York City of Neapolitan parents, Sal Pergola is a stocky, colorful, energetic man with an instinctive affinity for problems relating to tough East Side boys. He could throw an arm about a boy churning with resentment against some teacher and make him smile and feel ashamed, or he could berate another in a voice that could be heard halfway down the corridor; and the boys always had the feeling that he was one of them, trying to help them in his own way. They could no more think of hating Sal Pergola than they could think of hating an older brother.

By his amazing insight into the character of young men, he was able to penetrate the confidence of a youth who was the leader of one of the toughest neighborhood gangs in East Harlem. By long talks, Sal Pergola ultimately diverted this boy's interest from gangs and street fighting to an interest in his own future. He became one of the leaders in our civic projects and graduated with honors—all through the efforts of an understanding teacher and administrator.

Sal always likes to tell the story of his father, who in Italy had been an army officer and never lost his feeling for discipline. Sal could go out nights as a young man, but he always had to be back at a certain time. One night he returned about a half hour late. His father fetched him a terrific cuff on the side of his head. "This time I am going to forgive you," he shouted. He gave him another clout. "Next time I will not be so lenient.". . .

The antagonism of a public living outside the confines of East Harlem and the attacks of newspapers seeking sensational "blackboard-jungle" copy could only be countered by knowledge of the facts. I held frequent consultations with Dr. Thrasher and other sociologists at New York University, where I continued to teach the course on the social background of the Italian immigrant. For the purpose of attacking this community problem at Franklin, we began early to enlist the cooperation of churches, settlement houses, and civic organizations.

I walked into my office one morning to find a rather brash young man waiting for me. It was during Mussolini's Ethiopian campaign in 1935. Upon introducing himself as a reporter for one of the New York dailies, he asked, "Would you say, Mr. Covello, that there has been an increase in racial antagonism between the Negro and Italian since the start of this war?"

I looked at him in amazement. The reporter smiled. "This is a question of the black race and the white race. We know there have been incidents all over Harlem. How do you handle the problem at Benjamin Franklin?"

I tried to control my anger. Over at her desk, my secretary, Marge Banzello, caught my eye as if she thought he was out of his mind. Instead of saying what I wanted to, I answered, "I don't know what you are talking about. There is no identification between my students and the Ethiopian War. I doubt if they feel anything at all."

"And I doubt if our readers would believe that."

"Your readers can believe what they want to believe," I said. "If they want to believe that the streets of East Harlem are running with blood, that's their business. And if your paper wants to help them believe it that's your business. But I can assure you that there is absolutely no truth in this rumor." A happy thought occurred to me. I conducted the reporter out of the office and downstairs to the gymnasium.

There were a dozen or so boys practicing basketball, among them several colored students.

At the sight of us the boys stopped playing, one of the basketballs poised in the hands of a lanky Negro youth ready to shoot. I motioned to him, "Bob, come here!" Then I picked out the white boy nearest him, an Italian by the name of George Castelli. "You too, George."

"Now then," I said as both boys stood waiting, "this gentleman is a newspaper reporter. He wants to know if the war in Ethiopia has made any difference in the way you two boys feel about each other."

"Ethiopia?" Castelli echoed.

The Negro boy said, "What have I got to do with those people over there?" He put his hand on Castelli's shoulder. "This boy is my friend. That's all I know."

The reporter went away without his story. I did not bother to read the paper the next day to see if he had made one up. . . .

❖   ❖   ❖

The plan for the community program had been worked out during the summer of 1935 [in meetings] with . . . the chairman of our Social Studies Department and . . . the law secretary of the Board of Education. . . . The result of our summer conferences was the creation of the Community Advisory Council of Benjamin Franklin High School, whose membership consisted of representatives from civic and social agencies and community leaders from East Harlem and Yorkville.

In a community such as East Harlem of the thirties, composed primarily of foreign-born parents and American-born children, the most critical period in the life of the family was, we felt, that in which the children reach and live through adolescence. It is the age when the so-called American idea of "living one's own life" begins to clash with the European idea of family solidarity, of obedience and respect for elders, and of subservience to family needs and requirements.

The real educational problem among the Italians and Jews of yesterday and the Puerto Ricans of today lies in the emotional conflicts that are particularly tormenting to the boy whose parents are deeply oriented by centuries of foreign tradition and custom. The feeling of scorn and shame that builds in these children because of the pressure of adverse opinion from outside often produces antisocial attitudes dangerous to the boy and to the community—in short, the delinquent.

There was no denying the fact that outside the school there were vital, powerful, and compelling forces constantly educating the boys and girls of the community in spite of, or contrary to, the school ideal. On one side the community's motion picture houses, its dance halls, its streets, its gangs, and on the other its churches, its community houses, its welfare agencies, its law-enforcement agencies—these could either promote or destroy the work of the school. And the school itself had to be both leader and coordinating agency, to a certain extent the pivot upon which much even of the social and civic life would turn.

Almost immediately the council in cooperation with the Works Progress Administration set up an afternoon community playground from three-thirty until six P.M. for the children of the neighborhood. Next, an evening community center for adults, open from seven-thirty to ten P.M., was established, in an effort to place all the facilities of the school at the service of its neighbors. We also had an evening center for teenagers. All this was in addition to our regular evening elementary-school classes.

Every Wednesday night I was available in my office in the main building to anyone who wanted to see me for any purpose whatever. We called this Wednesday Night Principal's Conference. . . .

One night I invited an older student and his girl to have coffee with me after the usual conferences were over. On such occasions I was host, serving coffee and the cookies Rose always baked for me. This particular boy was a barrel-chested Italian by the name of Lupino, who in his early school career had caused the dean and teachers a great deal of trouble by fighting in the corridors and disrupting his classes. When he felt like it, he would get up and walk out of the class-room and return at his convenience. He was so rugged and powerfully built that few dared provoke him. Finally, after repeated trips to the dean's office, the dean brought him to me with a note from his teacher. "This trouble-maker is more than I can stand. I do not want him in my class."

I had talked with Lupino before. Underneath the characteristic sulking and resentful attitude of a boy in trouble, something else struggled for release. There was a feeling of life that was irrepressible and would not be chained. After letting him sit in a corner of the office for a while, I finally looked up from my desk and said, "All right. What is it this time?"

"You know. You got the report."

"I want you to tell me."

"That English teacher! She hates my guts. It seems everybody in this place hates my guts!"

"Just a minute," I said. "Come over here next to the desk. Don't shout. When you shout I can't hear anything. Now then, in a low voice, what were you saying?

Lupino shrugged. "What's the use? When something goes wrong I'm right there to get the blame. Know what I mean?"

"You mean you were born unlucky?"

"That's me all right. You can say that again."

"And you can say that this time your bad luck carried you right out of school because that is what the dean wants and that is what your teacher wants. And, unless I'm very much mistaken, that's what you want."

Lupino shook his head vigorously. This was not what he wanted at all. He wanted to finish high school. Even if it killed him there had to be one member of his family who graduated. It was just that he was unlucky.

I had often come upon this particular contradiction. I turned in my swivel chair. "I know how it is," I said to him. "You know what you want inside, only somehow you act just the opposite. Your mind gets away from you. Before you know it you've forgotten what the teacher is talking about. And when she catches you, you get mad. But you're not really mad at the teacher, you're mad at yourself."

Lupino considered a moment. "It certainly looks like I'm in a mess," he said.

"You certainly are. And at your age it's the kind of mess that will wind you up in jail. But why should you worry? It's what everyone expects. Your teachers. The dean. You yourself, for that matter. It would not surprise anybody, probably not even your mother and father. Another East Harlem kid going wrong."

Lupino dug his hands into his pockets. He tried to say something and then his lips clamped together.

"This time I haven't any choice, I've got to expel you. How can I run a school like this? How can anyone who wants to learn make any headway with you in the class?"

With almost superhuman effort to put down his pride, Lupino said, "Please, Pop, I've got to finish high school."

I was in a spot. I would have to appease the dean and the teacher. If he made more trouble it would be on my neck and I told him so. Besides his mother and father were Italian, and it would look as though I were making an exception.

"I promise," Lupino begged. "This time I give you my word of honor I won't let you down, Pop. I promise on the soul of my dead grandmother!"

I thought awhile. Then I said, "I don't know. Let me think about it. Go home and come back tomorrow morning."

The dean proved to be no particular problem. Though often severe in his punishment, he had a basic instinct for handling boys and knew his job. The teacher, however, was another matter. She was young, new to East Harlem, and could not wait to be reassigned to a school in a better neighborhood. I knew it without her telling me. She had been raised in Pelham, a peaceful suburb of New York, and this was her first regular job. While by sheer strength of character she could hold a class of my East Harlem boys together, Lupino was too much for her. After a few moments in my office, she broke down and started to cry. "It's as if he ridicules me. He's utterly contemptuous of everything I say. There in class I'm always conscious of his presence, like some animal ready to pounce on me. I've never handled such a student. Tell me, Mr. Covello, how do you do it?"

Her appeal was almost pathetic, as if I had some magic formula I could give her. "I don't know," I said. "It's easier for me, I guess, because I was raised the same way and have lived all my life in the same neighborhood. But then there are other women teachers who come from other parts of the city who understand the boys too. I don't know what it is, exactly. I do know, however, that if you convince yourself deep down that these boys, Lupino included, are basically not much different from others you have known, and that they would like to be liked by you, then most of your troubles will be over."

As for Lupino, I told her not to concern herself about him. "If he disturbs you or the class in the least way, just let me know. He'll be out of here that very day. But let's give him another chance. I know we can straighten him out." After she had gone, I sent for Lupino and made him write out a statement to the effect that at the very first adverse report he would voluntarily expel himself from school.

Lupino kept his word. He graduated a few years later. I never had cause to regret what I had done for him. Nor had his teachers, for that matter.

One night Lupino came to present me to his girl, Dolly, who lived on the same block and whom he had known most of his life. He told me he was working in a garage. "I like fooling around cars. In a couple of years when I've got some money saved, we'll get married, Dolly and me. Then I'll save some more and pick up a gas station and repair service someplace. That's what we got figured out." He patted the girl's hand and smiled. "How's that strike you, Pop? How's that for old Lupino who you thought was headed for the clink?"

Lupino's conversation touched on the neighborhood problems. "Boy, these kids today. I'm telling you, Pop. I saw a bunch of them just yesterday, breaking bottles and emptying garbage cans on the street. I said, 'Hey, whatsamatter with you guys? You got sawdust for brains or something? Even a bird don't foul its own nest.' "

After we had finished the coffee, Dolly rose to gather the cups and saucers and bring them to the washstand in a corner behind a screen. I made her sit down. "Oh, no," I said. "You are a guest here. He'll wash the dishes," pointing to Lupino.

Lupino bellowed like a bull.

"What's the matter with you, Pop? You wanna spoil my wife before I even get married?"

"Wash the dishes. It'll do you good. At home I help my wife. It's about time you started to learn."

I will always remember that hulk of a boy named Lupino—Lupino, the terror of 108th Street, who could probably lick any two boys in the school put together. He was not a student every teacher would be proud of. He would never set the world on fire and the school would never inscribe his name on its honor roll. At best he would own a garage and raise a family, that's all. But when he picked up those dishes and said to his girl, "This Pop Covello, he sure is one for the book!" I knew all over again why it was that I was a school teacher.

❖   ❖   ❖

Meanwhile the need for more room outside of the school building which we could use particularly over weekends for meetings and special classes became pressing. After a meeting of the Community Advisory Council one night, one of the PTA members, Mrs. Anna Russo, who lived next door to the school, came to my office. "We have a wonderful idea, Mr. Covello. All the empty stores in the block! Why couldn't we get some of these old stores, clean them up and fix them over, and use them like classrooms? "

"That's an extraordinary idea," I exclaimed, "if it's possible."

"You just leave everything to us," Mrs. Russo said. "We'll find out how it can be done."

This was the beginning of our unique "store fronts" or "street units" as we called them.

The owner of the building next to the school was willing to give us the use of a store, rent free for the first year. I inspected the store with Mrs. Russo. It was dirty beyond imagining and hopelessly in need of repair. My natural inclination was to turn aside from the unpleasant task of making it serviceable—postpone action. A few days later, Mrs. Russo returned, saying that the landlord now was willing to give us the use of the adjoining stores and that he would also permit the removal of the partition between the two.

These stores were even dirtier than the first. Though the space was now adequate, I still avoided making a commitment. I continued to inspect the premises with Mrs. Russo and some other PTA mothers. A crowd began to join us from the street. "Hey, Pop, what goes on?" one of the men from a plumbing shop asked.

"We're trying to figure out if we could clean up this mess and make a neighborhood meeting place," I said. "It looks hopeless."

"Ain't nuthing hopeless, Pop. You know that better'n any of us."

Several men offered to tear down the partition and do the plastering. The janitor of the building said he'd keep the place clean when the work was done. The women promised to take care of the furnishings and decoration. Everyone seemed anxious to have the club and eager to get started. "All right," I said. "Today is Tuesday. Saturday morning we will begin."

I returned to my office at the school, lingering doubts still in my mind. At lunch time I told my colleagues, Dr. Guerra and Mike Decessare about the arrangements. Both were as skeptical as I with regard to the work getting done.

It was May. Saturday was hot and humid. Of the men who had offered their services, only one showed up, and he did not have any tools. I managed to borrow a hammer and a piece of pipe that could be used for a crowbar and we started to hack away at the partition. As we sweated, the usual crowd began to gather in the doorway. Mrs. Russo and the women appeared. They began to upbraid the idlers.

"Aren't you ashamed, just standing there?

"You'll be the first to use this club after everybody else has done the work."

Sheepishly the men began to grin. A few of them moved inside. One of them took the piece of pipe from my hands. "This ain't work for you, Professor. You got brains to operate with. Here, let me have that thing."

The spirit caught on. Work gathered momentum. People mysteriously appeared from all over the neighborhood. When some of the students offered to lend a hand they were shooed away to their Saturday games and activities. I was thrust aside, given the dubious, strictly honorary title of "supervisor," while the artisans of the neighborhood took over.

The assistant to the janitor scraped away all the dirty wallpaper and washed the walls clean. The Jefferson Post of the American Legion sent men to replace the broken sink and patch up plaster. Women of the PTA donated the money with which to buy paint. Though the work was well in progress, there were those who doubted that the club would ever amount to anything. Even when the Works Progress Administration furnished us a social director in the person of a stately, blue-eyed woman from Georgia by the name of Mary Carter Winter, some still argued that she would be sitting inside the store all day long, reading a newspaper and watching the crowds go by.

The painting was not quite finished. There were loose boards in the floor to be repaired, furniture to be acquired, curtains to be hung, a hundred-and-one details before an official opening. Yet, whenever Mrs. Winter entered the store for one reason or another, children trooped in at her heels and stood around waiting for something to happen. Mrs. Winter began to talk to them of books and tell them stories while she sat on a wooden box and they gathered around her on the floor. Before anyone realized it she was running an open house for the children of the block.

Women donated odds and ends of furniture. Mrs. Redmond, chairman of our Music Department, contributed a piano, a large mirror, and some chairs and tables. Some of this furniture needed paint to freshen it up, and a group of the high-school boys insisted that this would be their contribution. They were working at this task one evening when I happened by. All the boys were fond of Mrs. Winter, but a few of them thought her a trifle simple-minded with respect to the ways of a city jungle like East Harlem. Unobserved for the moment, I listened to a lad of seventeen give her advice as he put a few finishing strokes of paint to a chair. "You don't know it, ma'am, but you got guys in here who don't belong in here."

"I don't understand what you mean," Mrs. Winter answered. "This is going to be a club for friends and neighbors. You must not talk about friends and neighbors in this manner."

"That's right," a younger boy said indignantly, "who don't belong in here!"

The boy who was painting smiled cynically. "I know what I'm talking about and you don't. Right here you've got guys who will steal things—grab stuff that don't belong to them. I know, because I'm one of them. And there's that one. And that. And that," singling out three others standing around.

Mrs. Winter was silent. The boys now all looked at her, intent, an interesting study, ready to deny direct accusation, waiting to be attacked individually and, at the same time, trying to appear indifferent about the club. Mrs. Winter turned once more to the youth with the paint brush. "Now we know how things stand. All you have to do is watch each other. You will have to watch each other because I won't have the time. Nor will anyone else, for that matter."

Such was the beginning of the Friends and Neighbors Club.

In the seven years of its existence, of the countless articles contributed to the club, rarely was anything damaged or stolen.

We soon discovered that people who would never dream of going near the school, feeling self-conscious, would make use of the facilities of the store fronts—making us further realize the need for small social and educational centers scattered around a neighborhood to supplement the work of the main building in community education. There were several workmen in the neighborhood who liked to sing. They would not think of setting foot in the school building, but Mrs. Redmond got them to organize a singing group and twice a week they never failed to be with us.

Soon after, out of another vacant store we made a library. One of the retired old men of the neighborhood took over the job of librarian. There were books for young and old in three languages, Italian, Spanish, and English, donated by our many friends. The library was followed by another unit for the Franklin Alumni Association, another for the Italian Educational Bureau which I had transferred from Columbia, and still another for the beginning of our work among Puerto Ricans.

During the period from 1936 to 1942, before the school moved to its new location on the East River Drive, we had five separate street units in operation, all maintained—with the exception of a very few salaried personnel—by independent funds raised through special drives and campaigns, dances, dinners, and social functions. . . .

❖   ❖   ❖

From the very first, the 1,800 boys who had been transferred from De Witt Clinton to form the student body of Benjamin Franklin could not reconcile themselves to the idea of continuing their high-school days in the two old elementary-school buildings that were originally annexes of Clinton. They had envisioned that when they became "upper termers" they would enjoy the beautiful new Clinton building and athletic grounds at Mosholu Parkway at the northern end of the Bronx. "We must be step-children here in East Harlem," they commented among themselves.

The boys deplored this state of affairs in the school newspaper, *The Franklin Almanac.* They even published an angry open letter to Mayor La Guardia.

> The City of New York promised its citizens a new high school to relieve the sorely overcrowded classes which were in existence at the time. Until this late date the city has not made good this promise. . . . We appeal to you as the Mayor to remember the forgotten promise which the people have not overlooked and as a citizen of the district in which Franklin is situated, we call upon you to support the movement to wipe out this disgrace to a community's dignity. . . .

The many efforts expended toward obtaining a new building finally proved successful. At about the time the housing project was terminated, the Board of Education made the necessary appropriation for the new school. There was great excitement, particularly when the building division submitted five possible locations. Four of these locations were in the tumble-down tenement section of East Harlem, and the fifth, the most desirable one, on 116th Street on the East River Drive. On this site the boys set their hearts. . . .

At the ground-breaking ceremonies for the new building, two young girls representing the school children of the city took part. One, Christina Claxton, was a descendant of Benjamin Franklin and the other, Rita Aluto, was the daughter of immigrant parents. Along with the Mayor, the Superintendent of Schools, and the Borough President of Manhattan, the girls each made a brief statement. Christina Claxton said, "I wish my great ancestor could be here today. He would be glad to see gathered together, as members of one group, young men whose fathers came from so many countries." Rita Aluto added, "The good things of life that you and I enjoy we owe to all God's children of every color, and nation, and creed."

After his own address, Mayor La Guardia took off his coat and turned the first shovel of earth on the school site. The eighteen hundred members of the student body and the hundreds of gathered spectators started to cheer, while the Father Duffy Cadets struck up a march. It was a moment I shall never forget.

It took two years to complete the new building. During this time we were living in a brownstone house just a few blocks away. On my way home from the old school at 108th Street, I would stop to watch the work which progressed with exasperating slowness. "I can't understand it," I would say to Rose. "At the rate they're going I'll be ready to retire before they finish."

I was not alone in my concern. The boys from the camera club who used to take photographs at various stages of the job would complain to me, "What goes on, Mr. Covello? They building Rome all over again?"

Slowly but surely the building took shape, and its beauty began to lift the spirits of all of us, not only those of us who were to occupy its halls but also the people who lived within the boundaries of its influence. We could begin to realize the words of Franklin when he wrote, "If a man empties his purse into his head, no man can take it away from him. An investment in knowledge always pays the best interest."

Dedication of our new high-school building was held in April of 1942, the week of the one-hundredth anniversary of the Board of Education. Classical in design, reminiscent of the architecture of the later colonial period, the school was built at a cost of three and one-half million dollars and was considered one of the most beautiful in the city. Thousands attended the ceremony, but it was not the happy occasion we had hoped for. Between the breaking of ground and the completion of the building, war had been declared.

War colored the entire ceremony that day. Mayor La Guardia reminded the boys that whether or not the war ended before they could serve in it, they would face another war against dislocated conditions and that they had to bring themselves to realize the enormity of their responsibilities and prepare for them.

As I stood up on the platform of our magnificent auditorium, capable of seating thirteen hundred people, facing my students, my friends and neighbors of East Harlem, I could hardly speak. "To those of us who have lived and worked in this community for many years," I said, "this occasion marks the fulfillment of a long cherished dream—the dream of transforming dirt and ugliness into spaciousness and beauty, of bringing light into darkness. . . ."

In speaking about the program of the school, I added, "Fulfilling the ideal of Community Service to which it has been dedicated, the Benjamin Franklin High School will now operate on a round-the-clock program of use by all community organizations. Believing that a school building should be available to all the members of the community, all the time, the Board of Education has conferred a signal honor on Benjamin Franklin High School.

"By a special vote it has decreed that our building is to be open every hour of every day of the year. This means that we who live and work in East Harlem are free to use its magnificent resources at all times.". . .

❖   ❖   ❖

The racial incident [a fight] receded into the limbo of a half-forgotten nightmare. In a few weeks there was hardly anything to indicate that it had ever happened, as far as the school was concerned. I moved about the building, watching the boys in class, in the lunchrooms, talking together in the corridors, Negro and white, and it was heartening to see how every trace of animosity had been cast aside. We were back once more in the normal healthy routine of Franklin. The only difference was that now we knew better than ever that the story of the community school in East Harlem had to be told beyond its own boundaries. If we were misrepresented again, great harm would come of it. For no man can revile his less fortunate neighbor without weakening the entire fabric of a democratic society. And no man is safe unless all men are safe.

By complaining about the sensational treatment newspapers too often give various school situations, I do not mean to suggest that we had no delinquency at Benjamin Franklin. In the same measure that we had crime in East Harlem, an admittedly and understandably "tough" section of New York, we had delinquency at Franklin. But we never let it get out of control. We treated the rough boys in the only way they could understand—firmly—and they respected us for it. We never considered a boy hopeless unless he was implicated in a serious crime, in which case it was no longer the school's business but the law's. Quite frankly, we kept the police out of our school problems with so-called delinquents until we had absolutely no other choice. Always we followed two cardinal principles: get to the boy, make him feel that we represented hope; and go to the family to dig for the root of the problem.

I remember literally hundreds of boys sitting tongue-tied, frustrated, doubled up inside with shame and confusion in my office. For many of them we went to court, to police stations, to hospitals, interceding for another chance. But to intercede is to assume responsibility.

We got jobs, "big brothers," psychological and welfare help. We tried to give them a mixture of discipline and affection. How well I recall our successes and our failures. As I look back today, these are my joys and my sadnesses. . . .

Today's teenage gang members seem to carry a frightening arsenal of guns and knives, if newspaper reports are accurate. In my time at Franklin, the majority of boys carried the ordinary pocket knife, and, on more than one occasion, teachers and I were able to confiscate the villainous looking "switchblades" from boys who were seen displaying them. But I can honestly say that in all my experience as a high-school principal in East Harlem, I do not recall that a knifing took place in the school.

In the collection of knives and assorted weapons, which were confiscated, was a murderous pair of brass knuckles fitted with sharp spikes taken from a boy caught clowning with them in the hall with some of his companions. I'll never forget Tony Zucco. Stubborn as a mule. When I got him in my office he refused to tell me where he had obtained the brass knuckles.

"I just can't tell you, Pop. I just can't."

It was exasperating. I couldn't pry the story out of him. I finally had to let him go. After he finished school he became a cab driver, and I used to see him every now and then in the neighborhood. When I mentioned the brass knuckles he always became vague and avoided the subject. Not very long ago I asked him point blank. "Come on, Tony. It's years now. Tell me the truth about the knuckles."

He grinned, scratched his head, and told me the truth. "I found them in a garbage can. I never used them, but I couldn't tell you that, Pop. It was too tame. A tough kid like me, naw!". . .

My many years at Franklin made me believe more firmly than ever in . . . the opportunity for boys to pursue their education far beyond the limitations sometimes imposed upon them because of the character of the neighborhood in which they happen to be born.

In the creation of Franklin, we argued for a cosmopolitan or comprehensive high school; and when plans for the new Franklin building were under way, we again urged a broad, all-inclusive educational program that would meet the needs and interests of all types of students. In addition to the academic course, we argued for a general course, a commercial course enriched by the industrial arts, and also a vocational or trade course for those students who wanted it. We definitely did not want just a trade school. We wanted to eliminate the sharp distinctions between the different types of high schools which, in my opinion, create social cleavages and develop a type of class consciousness that is the very antithesis of democracy.

It is interesting to note that 40 to 50 per cent of Franklin graduates now make applications to enter colleges or universities. A vocational or trade school would have restricted many of these boys in their preparation for higher education.

The high school has now become the common school of America and it is here where all American youth should mingle and rub elbows, get to understand and appreciate each other—the academic student who plans for college, the student who plans for a business career, and the student whose inclinations and abilities direct him to the skilled trades. This to me represents one of the basic functions of our American high school.

❖   ❖   ❖

Compulsory retirement meant that in the not-too-distant future my work as a high-school principal would be over. No matter how I tried I could not visualize myself separated from the neighborhood and the work which had been my life. All that I had learned about the immigrant and his child in the struggle to become part of American society I could not shelve or lock up in a desk drawer simply because a prescribed number of years had marched by. What happens to the mind which remains alert after the law dictates that its owner can no longer work? What happens to the heart that continues to reach out to those who are still in a new land? . . .

My days as a high-school teacher and principal are over. My mind and my heart, however, are with the boys I taught for close to half a century. In these pages I have sought to give a picture of these years. I have tried to show how, though at first I was only concerned with books and the imparting of information, ultimately I came to realize how the heart and mind not only of the individual boy but of his whole community are involved in the education process.

There are those, I am sure, who will argue that I have painted too glowing a picture of the boys whose lives began in the slums of Manhattan, that I should have made more of violence, of juvenile delinquency, and of social chaos. It is so easy to concentrate on the sensational event in the life of a community and to ignore the everyday pattern of living of the thousands of families that struggle to raise their children decently against tremendous odds. I could have recalled some of the criminal types I have known, the drug addicts, the boys who contrary to expectations suddenly went wrong. I could have recorded many unpleasant things, but I did not. I did not because I felt it was necessary to emphasize the positive and not dwell on the ugly; for the ugly in our day and age receives all too much emphasis. This is not and never was the way I looked upon my job as a teacher. My approach was determined by the fact that in the most difficult boy I always saw another side. I sensed beneath the rough, defiant, and cynical attitude the yearning for appreciation, understanding, and the willingness to struggle to become an accepted member of society. I felt that the difficult boy—yes, even the young criminal, was more sinned against than sinning. We, as adults, do not come to him with clean hands and clear consciences because too often we have failed to help him live by the moral code that we write and preach. I know too that of the almost one million school children in New York City, regardless of national origin, race, or creed, only a small per cent constitute a social and community problem—a menace to themselves and to society.

As a teacher I have witnessed the antisocial behavior that has led to delinquency and worse, and have had the frustrating experience of lacking the resources to arrest or divert it. And so have hundreds of my fellow teachers.

What I did want to stress is that an overwhelming number of boys, in spite of living in difficult communities, with many demoralizing influences, have made fine lives for themselves and are among our civic leaders today.

Not long ago I attended the annual conference of the Council of Spanish-American Organizations which was held at the Benjamin Franklin High School. Fifty-eight separate organizations met and spent the day discussing the problems of their people and what they were doing about them. The theme was "We Help Ourselves." The idea for this council was originated and worked out by Joe Monserrat, its first president, who claims that it was his early experiences at Franklin that gave him the training and desire to work for the good of his fellow American citizens from Puerto Rico.

There are so many heartening examples among the young men who graduated from Franklin which prove that in order to develop civic-mindedness and a willingness to serve, the process must begin as the boys grow up in the school. No better example can I give you of the importance of high-school boys sharing in the responsibility of improving community living than to quote several passages from a letter which I received during the Second World War from Elmer Glaser, a Jewish boy of an immigrant family who graduated from Franklin in 1937 not only with high honors but with the affection of the whole school.

> If the only function of school in these times were to teach the "three R's" I would say better to close them, saving time, money, and effort. . . . But the place of school in society is far greater, and I can hardly believe that this would have to be demonstrated again.
> . . .

I don't have to tell you about how the inspiration of us Franklin students was fired by the thought that we would be able to participate in something bigger than ourselves that would allow us to translate into action some of the things we had been hearing about and seeing in books. "Democracy" was a little abstract and far away in meaning to most of us. It had begun in 1776, it had an annual ritual each November, and there were guardians of it in Washington.

Almost overnight, it meant something concrete and very close. Part of it meant that I, born of a people that has been discriminated against and persecuted for many years, could meet with other common everyday people from all walks of life and discuss ideas for solving problems we all shared. . . .

I helped older people organize meetings, learned how to write letters, how to make contacts.

We met in the auditorium, heard our committee progress reports, sang together (I'm chromatic monotone), listened to speakers, and in general enjoyed those bonds of fellowship and good will that are rare and when they are found one long remembers. Sometimes I had the privilege to address these gatherings.

Here I met and spoke with neighborhood doctors, trade-union members, priests, teachers, housewives, storekeepers, and others, and education suddenly became meaningful to me, drawing out any talents I had along the lines of writing, speaking, organizing, and so on. This was a change from the routine classroom lecture-and-regurgitation method of education. . . .

My work on community affairs was done mostly after "school hours" but instead of losing out in my studies, I came to class next day with renewed interest in matters under study and a burning desire to learn. A lesson in immigration policy was no longer a matter of arbitrary arithmetic formulae, but a flesh and blood policy that dealt with matters of life and death and freedom and tyranny for the people I had mingled with at Community Night, or last night. The discussion of housing problems really amounted to if and when and how were the people of East Harlem going to have decent homes instead of the dark, dank tenements I had seen last week when I made the rounds with a petition for a housing project for the neighborhood. . . .

I merely wanted to tell you of my belief that I and many others profited individually from participation in the community program and that as a result of our collective efforts the community, and through it, the city and nation, have profited.

If I had nothing else besides this letter from Elmer Glaser to show the value of our experiment at Franklin in school–community education, I would feel well rewarded for the many years that I devoted to this cause.

A teacher is fortunate in that he is left with so many wonderful—if intangible—mementos. A young man named Joe Roberto is now supervising architect of the new Rockefeller Dorado Hotel project in Puerto Rico. He was a Clinton graduate of around the year 1927. I had heard of his work as an architect long before he became associated with Rockefeller. A surprise telephone call at Benjamin Franklin brought us together two or three years ago for an hour or so as he was passing through on his way to California. As I showed him around our beautiful building he confided to me something I had never known. "Pop," he said, "have you any idea how I happened to become an architect?"

He told me that it all started in that tiny office of mine at De Witt Clinton while he was operating the mimeograph machine and I was talking to one of the other boys who wanted to become a draughtsman.

"I never forgot what you said to this kid. You said, 'Why do you want to settle for draughtsman? That's more or less mechanical. Anybody can become a draughtsman. Set your goal high. Become an architect. Try for the top.'"

Joe Roberto smiled. "You weren't talking to me at all, but I'm the one who was affected. From that day on I began to dream of one day becoming an architect."

Just the other day I received a postal card from Joe from Puerto Rico. He finds himself perfectly at home down there. "Doctor, you recognized the fine qualities of these people long before I did. They are best in the knowledge of their craft—masonry, tile work, plaster, and concrete. I thought only the Italians had mastered this art."

The fundamental objectives and the moral ideal are constant. It is the human patterns of behavior which are changeable and must be adjusted to achieve these objectives, for the most stupendous fact of human existence is that man *can* change, for good or for ill. Man has over the centuries made many attempts to achieve the objectives of a higher moral code. At times he failed. At other times he seemed almost to succeed. When some degree of success was achieved, it always appeared to be based on one of the most fundamental bases of human behavior—faith. Faith in the world; faith in man. For the struggle of man to achieve the ideals of a moral world will never suffer permanent discouragement.

What was applicable to me as a child in the little Italian mountain town of Avigliano holds just as firm today; the child must be inculcated with a responsibility toward his family, his elders, and the community in which he lives. In turn, every member of the community has a responsibility toward that child. Only thus can there be progress in the development of the useful citizen.

"The student must suffer," my uncle, the priest, used to say to me over sixty years ago. That also has truth today, despite educators who have advocated the "no-failing theory" and the concept of uninhibited self-expression. For, how is it possible to inculcate discipline—self-discipline—and develop the desire to improve in a child if he is not taught a sense of duty and responsibility along with his rights and privileges.

Yet I do not believe in beating lessons into boys. Far from it. "Foolishness is tied up in the heart of a boy," the proverb says, "the rod is what will remove it from him." This "get tough" idea which seems to be gathering momentum in some quarters today proves only that man has a short memory. The severity of punishment practiced in days gone by neither corrected, nor reformed, nor lessened delinquency and crime. I never found it necessary to lay hands on a boy. I know that corporal punishment is not the answer. However, I am convinced that a firm hand when the child is young is the best method for instilling in him a normal and healthy attitude toward life and living in the society of his fellow human beings.

The increasingly serious problem of juvenile crime that exists today cannot be shrugged off. Yet we must not use the schools and the teachers as scapegoats. We must search within ourselves for the fault and the solution. Adolescents are hardly responsible for the world they grow up in, or for the influences which shape their lives. One need not seek far to find an environment which successfully controls the adolescent: in Chinese communities in this country, where respect for family and tradition amounts almost to religion, there is no such thing as juvenile delinquency. And these are usually low-income, often tenement, communities.

It is ironical but true that the years of the great depression and immediately following were the most productive in our Benjamin Franklin experiment. Because of the unemployment situation, many capable WPA workers worked without cost to us on our numerous community programs. Bitter irony indeed! Workers in a depression made possible what today is practically out of the question. With a national budget in the billions, we still sorely neglect the education of our young people. The great majority of people refuse to face reality. Education costs money. While they may pay the idea lip service, their minds refuse to grasp the fact that there are just not enough teachers and that they are not paid enough for the significant work they do. At least a part of the answer is as simple as that. The Russians accepted this fact when they decided to give their teachers the same status and pay that they give their doctors.

I believe and will always believe in the potential in every boy to lead a good and useful life—if we as adults will only care enough, take the time and the trouble and the expense to develop this potential. The great boys I have known—Benny Segreto, Le Count Russel, Hans Geissler, Elmer Glaser, Joe Monserrat, Vito Marcantonio, and hundreds more—exist in all boys.

The teacher is the heart of the educational process and he must be given the opportunity to teach—to devote himself whole-heartedly to his job under the best circumstances. Half a century as a teacher leads me to the conclusion that the battle for a better world will be won or lost in our schools.

About the Author

VITO PERRONE is a member of the learning and teaching faculty and director of teacher education at the Harvard Graduate School of Education. He has been a secondary school teacher of history and social studies and continues to be deeply involved in the life of elementary and secondary schools. He was a professor of history and dean of common learning and graduate studies at Northern Michigan University (1962–1968) and professor of history, education, and peace studies and dean of the New School and Center for Teaching and Learning at the University of North Dakota (1968–1986). In addition, Dr. Perrone has served since 1972 as coordinator of the North Dakota Study Group on Evaluation, a national organization of teachers, school administrators, community organizers, and university scholars. He has written extensively on issues such as educational equity, curriculum, progressivism in education, and testing and evaluation.